EVERY DOWN, EVERY DISTANCE

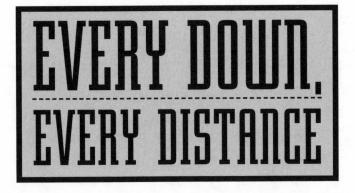

EVERY DOWN, EVERY DISTANCE

MY JOURNEY TO THE NFL

Wayne Chrebet

WITH VIC CARUCCI

D O U B L E D A Y
NEW YORK LONDON TORONTO SYDNEY AUCKLAND

PUBLISHED BY DOUBLEDAY
a division of Random House, Inc.
1540 Broadway, New York, New York 10036

DOUBLEDAY and the portrayal of an anchor with a dolphin are
trademarks of Doubleday, a division of Random House, Inc.

Library of Congress Cataloging-in-Publication Data

Chrebet, Wayne.
Every down, every distance: my journey to the NFL/Wayne Chrebet
with Vic Carucci.—1st ed.
p.   cm.
1. Chrebet, Wayne.   2. Football players—United States Biography.
I. Carucci, Vic.   II. Title.
GV939.C49A3   1999
796.332′092—dc21
[B]   99-30499
CIP

ISBN 0-385-49630-3

To Mom and Dad, there aren't enough words in the world to express how much you mean to me. Thanks for teaching me to never settle for anything less than the best. To Jennifer, I'm the luckiest guy in the world to have a sister as loving and caring as you; to my late Uncle Al and my Aunt JoAnn, cousins Jonathan and Rachel, and my Uncle Gabe, thanks for always being there; to Amy Wick, for your unselfish devotion to helping me fulfill my dreams. I'll love you forever for that. To Art Weiss, you're not only the best agent a player could have, but you and your family are like family to me; to my Grandma, Pauline Toth, you have been the inspiration behind my success and I know you are always watching over me.

And to everybody who bleeds green and white like I do. J-E-T-S! Jets! Jets! Jets!—W.C.

To Rhonda, the best friend a husband could have; to Kristen and Lindsay, who make fatherhood a true blessing.—V.C.

Acknowledgments

As with any worthwhile personal or professional accomplishment in both of our lives, we know that writing a book is a team effort.

So besides the many hours we spent together getting this thing on tape and then going over every word on paper, we relied on the generous and talented assistance of many others, several of whom shared our vision on this project.

First and foremost, we want to thank Shawn Coyne of Doubleday. He was the one who first believed that this story had to be told and that there were people out there who wanted to read it. He gave us a starting point and showed us the way to the finish line. His friendly voice, constant encouragement, eternal optimism, and deft editing were greatly appreciated. Kudos, as well, to his able assistants, Theresa Pulle and Chris Min.

We want to thank the Basil Kane Literary Agency for helping to put the wheels in motion once Shawn let it be known that this was a book he wanted to publish. Basil, no one in the business is your equal in terms of class, dignity, loyalty, and friendship.

Art Weiss is so much more than an attorney and sports agent. He is a friend, confidant, booster, and steadying force.

Besides his major role in the birth of the NFL career of a certain no-name kid from New Jersey, he also had a huge part in getting this book off the ground and bringing it in for a safe landing. Art was always only a phone call away to fill holes, check facts, locate photographs, share his wisdom, and take care of every little but critical detail.

Besides the collaboration that made this collaboration and the career that it covers possible, Wayne Sr. and Paulette Chrebet were as tremendously supportive in this venture as they have been in every aspect of their children's lives. You can't be thanked enough for sharing the stories, as well as your numerous scrapbooks and photo albums.

Not to mention your kindness and generosity.

Every brother should be so fortunate to have a sister as loving and devoted as Jennifer Chrebet. As a reporter for *People* magazine, she knows a thing or two about the process of telling a story in print. And a lot of that rubbed off on her brother through the years. Jennifer's memory and attention to detail were vital components to the interviewing, writing and revising processes.

Rhonda Carucci did her typically professional and flawless job of transcribing hours upon hours of tape-recorded book interviews, while still keeping up with the demands of being a mother and a wife. She also was there to provide support and helpful advice every step of the way.

We'd like to extend our gratitude and appreciation to Al Pereira of the New York Jets, Jim Sheehan of Hofstra University, Richard A. Brightly, Marty Lyons, Joe Traver, David M. Jones, and Brian M. Ballweg.

Thanks also to Ty Ballou and Melissa Heher of PLB Sports, Inc.; Lisa Platt; all of the good folks at the Fairfield Inn in East Rutherford, the Long Island Marriott Hotel and Conference Center, the Sheraton Meadowlands, the Sea Shack, and J. T. McToole's.

Wayne would be remiss if he didn't mention his closest friends who have been like brothers to him—Brian Clark, Carlos Garay, Tim Gray, Dave Saper, Chuckie Hawthorne, Jon Camera, and Chris Annibal—and his extended family, "Team 80."

And a very special thank you must go to Huff and the rest of the coaches at Garfield High, Hofstra University, and the New York Jets.

—Wayne Chrebet, Colts Neck, N.J.
—Vic Carucci, East Amherst, N.Y.

Wayne to Vic: I'd like to extend my gratitude to you and your wife, Rhonda, for helping me to tell my story and making it a pleasurable experience.

Vic to Wayne: Thanks for allowing me to help you tell your story and, most of all, for taking us into your wonderful family.

EVERY DOWN, EVERY DISTANCE

1

Sleepless
in Baltimore

Why am I here?

I asked myself that question—over and over—as I was lying in bed in a Baltimore hotel room.

It was the middle of the night. My eyes were wide open.

The calendar said it was April 1, 1995, but unfortunately, this was not the middle of some goofy April Fools' joke.

In only a matter of hours, the sun would be up and I would be at Johns Hopkins University for a tryout camp hosted by the Baltimore Stallions (known at the time as the Baltimore Football Club) of the Canadian Football League.

This was not to be confused with the NFL's annual scouting combine, which invites more than three hundred draft-eligible players in the country—as rated by league scouts—to spend a week at the RCA Dome in Indianapolis, showing their stuff to coaches, general managers, and scouts.

After finishing up a pretty good career as a wide receiver at Hofstra University, I thought I might get a chance to be among that top three hundred.

I guess my invitation got lost in the mail before it reached my parents' home in Wanaque, New Jersey.

I was one of about a hundred and ninety guys that paid fifty bucks each and signed an injury waiver so that members of the Stallions' player personnel department could see us. Their roster was already pretty well set from the team that had lost the 1994 Grey Cup to the British Columbia Lions on a last-second field goal, so it wasn't as if they were looking for a particular person to sign. It was like, no matter what you did, they were going to say, "Sorry, we're not interested."

How do you get up for something like that?

I had only gone to Baltimore because Kenny Colon, one of my fellow wide receivers at Hofstra, was going and asked if I wanted to come along. My CFL negotiating rights already belonged to the Hamilton Tiger-Cats, but the rules in that league were loose enough that the Stallions would have had no problem signing me if they wanted to.

Besides, I figured it might be worthwhile to show what I

could do in front of some pro football types, regardless of where they were from. At that time, my agent couldn't even get phone calls returned from something called the United Football Association, which I don't think ever played a game.

NFL teams were sending me nice warm letters like this one:

March 13, 1995

Dear Sir,

Thank you for your interest in the Philadelphia Eagles. We have received your film and statistical history and have reviewed it accordingly.

The college draft and the free agent market provide us with such a significant number of available players that it makes it impossible to offer tryouts to everyone who may desire one.

At this time, those players currently available to us are more in line with the caliber of player that we are looking for to fill the few roster spots that will become available.

Should you decide that you would like to further pursue playing in the NFL, you will find a card enclosed with the phone number for NFL International.

Best of luck in the pursuit of your future goals.

Sincerely,
John Wooten
Vice President/Director of Player Personnel
Philadelphia Eagles Football Club, Inc.

What he really was saying to me was: "Look, kid. We know, even without ever actually having scouted you, that you're not good enough for the NFL. Maybe you should see if you can cut it in our version of the minors, the World League of American Football, before you try to hang out with the big boys."

Once I got to Baltimore, I realized that what the Stallions were staging was just a giant meat market. The only thing missing was a USDA APPROVED stamp on my butt.

And the only thing I was going home with was a lost night of sleep.

That's because the night before I got up close and personal with one of the loudest, most annoying sounds I had ever heard in my life: my father's snoring! And I do mean SNORING!!!

Now, you have to understand that my dad, Wayne Sr., and I are as close as can be, so it was automatic that he was going to make this trip with me. Our relationship is much more like that of best friends than of a father and a son. We're buddies to the end. In fact, a lot of times I don't even call him Dad. I call him Dude.

I just had never given much thought to the sleeping arrangements in the hotel room we would be sharing. Kenny had one of the two beds, of course. That left Dad and me to share the other, something we had never done before as adults.

Believe me, it is something we will never do again.

Dad wasn't just snoring up a storm. He was snoring up a hurricane. The guy was making furniture move.

So as I was lying in bed, still staring into the darkness, I'd finally say, "Dude, you're killing me. I have got to sleep."

"I'm sorry," he'd say before turning over.

Then he'd start again five seconds later. And I'd be saying to myself, *Oh, man, come on* . . .

This went on all night. It was horrible. It was the closest I ever came to taking a whack at him.

I wound up standing in front of the window, watching the sun come up. Before I knew it, we were out the door and on the field. I was the piece of meat with the bags under his eyes, yawning. Had it not been so cold, I probably could have gone to sleep right there on the field.

The first clue that this was not a high-class operation was the fact we were given no warm-up. It was like: "OK, we want you to run this pattern . . . then run that drill . . . then run this drill . . ." If the idea was to see how many guys could pull their hamstrings in one morning, this was the perfect way to do it.

There must have been about twenty-five receivers out there. There were quarterbacks, but most of them didn't throw the ball as well as I was used to. Carlos Garay, my quarterback at Hofstra, had a great combination of strength and accuracy that was pretty hard to duplicate. Unfortunately, he wasn't there.

Like the other receivers, I was also working with these guys for the first time in my life, so there were obviously going to be timing problems. You would tell them the route you were going to run, but that didn't necessarily mean that you and the ball were going to end up in the same zip code, let alone the same spot on the field.

And the defensive backs were just mauling you every step of the way.

We were put through the standard speed, strength, and agility drills that you go through at any noncontact workout. But the Stallions did have a pretty unique way of measuring your vertical jump. At the NFL scouting combine, you have a metal pole attached to a base and metal slats stacked on top. Facing the pole, you make a standing jump and reach as high as you can to knock the slats with your hand, which precisely gauges how high you got off the ground. The Stallions? They used one of the stadium light posts at Johns Hopkins, marking various heights with pieces of athletic tape. Facing the post, you made a standing jump and the scouts tried to guess where your hand touched the tape. The problem was, your whole body wound up slamming into the post before your hand made contact.

Then one scout turned to the other and said, "Looks like thirty-five inches to me. What do you think?"

"Yeah, thirty-five sounds good."

I had on the pair of Nikes that I had worn during my senior season at Hofstra. They were really nice turf shoes, and I loved them. What happens the first time I make a plant while running a pass route? My right foot comes tearing out of the right side of the shoe. I had to switch to my dad's tennis shoes, which were too small and much better suited for gardening work than a football workout.

So let's review this wonderful trip. I spend a whole night listening to my father snore instead of sleeping. I'm freezing my butt off, waiting for twenty-four other receivers to take their turn in each drill. I'm slamming into a light post. I'm running one pattern, the quarterback is throwing another, and the defensive back is pounding on me through every step I take . . . all while wearing a pair of my father's gardening shoes.

And did I mention that this was going to lead to no-where?

All of a sudden, the thought of getting a degree and going to work in the nine-to-five world didn't sound so bad anymore.

When you're a big guy from a big college, you don't have to find NFL workouts; they find you. When you're a small guy from a small school, you pretty much have to beg just for an opportunity to get noticed.

That's where my father and Art Weiss, my agent and good friend, came in.

My dad had made a highlight videotape of all of my big plays from Hofstra. It was kind of crudely pieced together from his VCR recordings of Sports Channel's coverage of our games on cable TV. He called all thirty NFL teams at the time to get their addresses and the names of each player personnel direc-tor, then he put thirty copies of the tape in the mail. At that point, I don't think either of us expected it to lead to anything. We just wanted to see if it was a possibility.

If nothing happened, it was no big deal.

When Dad failed to get a single response, we hooked up with Art, who is from Franklin Lakes, New Jersey. Dad made another batch of tapes, only this time Art packaged each one with a cover letter and a two-page résumé with all of my major statistical accomplishments from college and high school, then he fired them off to every player personnel director and general manager at every level of pro football: the NFL, the CFL, the Arena League, the World League of American Football, and even the United Football Association.

The hope was that one of them just might see something that would merit a closer look.

That's the big advantage to getting invited to college all-star games and the combine—you don't have to tell the pro scouts you're out there because they already know about you. You're on the draft board of every team in the league. You're someone they won't easily forget.

It's no accident that about 90 percent of the players at the combine wind up in an NFL training camp, either as a draft pick or a free agent. And because you get tested in so many different areas, you're able to give teams a much more complete picture of the kind of player and person you are. This way the coach has some idea of what to expect from you in the conference championship when the score's tied and there are only a few ticks left on the clock.

When the heat's turned up like that, are you going to fold

like a lounge chair? Or are you going to come through in the clutch, like I saw Joe Montana do so many times against my New York Giants when I was a kid?

When you go to an all-star game, you get to practice in pads in front of the two NFL coaching staffs that are there to guide each team, as well as all of the other coaches, general managers, player personnel directors, and scouts from the rest of the league. You can show how you practice in front of a very critical audience, which is a good indicator of the type of player you are.

Then you can show how you play against some of the top talent in the country during the game. That's probably one of the best opportunities you can have if you're a player from a small school—to go against all of those guys from the bigger schools and see if you can make a dent.

But it was an opportunity I was never going to get. Hofstra had neither the reputation nor the experience to prepare players for the pros. Before I came along, the last member of the Flying Dutchmen to make an NFL roster was former Jet center John Schmitt—and that was in 1964.

Typical of the brick walls we kept running into was a phone conversation Art Weiss had with Art Haege, player personnel director for the Iowa Barnstormers of the Arena League. This guy had seen one of my highlight tapes.

He wasn't impressed.

"Yeah, I looked at the tape," Haege said. "And I'll tell you what. We can't use a kid like this. He's too small. He's too slow. It's just a guy we know wouldn't fit in."

"Well, how about sending it over to John Peterson?" my agent said, referring to the director of player personnel for the CFL's Toronto Argonauts.

"I could do that. But you're basically wasting your time."

As far as I know, the tape went no further, even though the Tiger-Cats would later include me on their negotiating list.

There were a lot of player personnel types who tried to tell Art that representing me was the biggest mistake of his career. As he later would put it, "I had so many doors slammed in my face, my nose was becoming flat. I had people laugh at me. I had people say to me, 'Whatever aspirations you have in this business, you're risking them if you stand behind this guy.' "

So if I was to have any chance of playing pro football, I pretty much had to settle for meat-market-style workouts like the one in Baltimore and the one a few weeks earlier that a New Mexico-based pro scouting service conducted in the Rutgers University practice bubble. For a hundred and twenty-five dollars, I got a T-shirt and a water bottle—and not a whole lot more.

The service has scouts that record your height, weight, forty-yard dash time, and your vertical jump. Then it circulates the results, along with a short videotape of your workout, to every pro football team, although it tends to do a better job of getting guys noticed by the Arena League and the CFL than the NFL.

The funniest thing about the people who run this service is that after I had had two productive seasons with the Jets, they started including my photo in their literature, as if to tell everyone that I was one of their "great finds." I'd have been more impressed with that if someone watching me that day had actually pulled me aside and said something—anything— about my workout.

As I recall it, I felt once again like I was part of a herd of cattle and that nothing I had done made them look at me as if I were anything other than one of the longest of long shots out there. I have a feeling the decision to put my photo on their literature was made when someone who happened to be going through the files discovered that I had attended that workout.

And, after all, they did give me that T-shirt and water bottle.

The most frustrating thing about most of these sessions is that they have absolutely nothing to do with football. You do a lot of running and a lot of jumping. You do almost no catching, blocking, tackling, or anything else that the teams are supposedly looking to hire you to do.

That just didn't make sense to me.

I realize it's important for scouts to see how you could run and jump and what kind of reflexes you have. But somewhere in there, I thought it might be nice to do something that involved football.

All of those workouts were humbling to a point, just because they didn't seem like they were going anywhere. The conditions aren't the best. At that time of year, the weather is pretty darn cold and damp in the Northeast.

You're also making things harder on yourself by pressing. Obviously, you don't want to drop a single pass; you don't want to run a bad route. Then what happens is that you start to think about what you're doing. And the worst thing you can do is *think* about something that comes so naturally to you because you're trying to overconcentrate.

The first time I worked out for the Jets—at their annual session to look at college seniors from the tri-state area—they didn't even have a football on the field. I was supposed to be there to show them what I could do as a wide receiver, and they didn't have any catching drills. They just wanted to get our times running ten-, twenty-, and forty-yard dashes.

"But catching the ball is what I do best," I said. "Why won't you let me catch passes for you?"

"Because we know you can catch the ball," one of their scouts said.

"What you're giving me is a track workout, and I'm not a track runner. I'm a good athlete. I can do any sort of running you want me to do. But if you give me a track workout, when it's all over, you're going to see: five-foot-ten, a hundred and eighty pounds, Hofstra, and my times in the ten, twenty, and forty. And that's it."

I did pretty well on the quickness and speed drills, but it was nothing to the point where they were going to say, "Watch out, Carl Lewis!"

At the time I knew that performance alone wasn't going to do me any good as far as hooking on with the Jets or any other team. Football's a contact sport, and I love contact. I wanted to put the pads on. I wanted to catch the ball. I wanted to show them that I could play this game well enough to be given a shot to make an NFL squad.

It was like: *These are the things I studied for—and they're not even on the test. What am I supposed to do?*

As always, the answer was: *Make the best of it, Wayne.*

Besides the one conducted by the Jets, I also went to regional workouts staged by the Carolina Panthers and Dallas Cowboys.

I was among the local college seniors that the Giants invited to what they call their annual Stadium Day. It isn't a workout. They just weigh you, show you their highlight film, then give you lunch. You never even set foot on the field— which would have been a dream come true at that point—but it was better than nothing.

At least at the Carolina workout, I was asked to run some routes and do some things that related to football, which included catching punts from the superpowerful leg of Todd Sauerbrun, who went to West Virginia and was from Long Island. No one was looking at me for my punt-return skills, but I was pretty proud of the fact that I was shagging the guy's towering kicks without any problem. After all, he did wind up being a second-round draft pick of the Chicago Bears.

I had Carlos throwing to me that day, which was to my advantage because he has a rocket for an arm and puts the ball right on the money. In fact, he was throwing so well in the workout that one of the scouts had to tell him to put the ball a little bit farther away from me to make it tougher to catch.

"Throw it high, then throw it low," the scout said. "Make him work for it."

So Carlos, who now plays in the Arena League, made me work. I just kept catching his passes.

The most satisfying workout of them all was the one I had for Jim Garrett, who scouted the New Jersey area for the Cowboys. Each year he gets together a group of college players at Red Bank, New Jersey.

The thing that impressed me about Jim was that he wasn't just sitting there with a stopwatch and a pad and pen. He was looking at us; he was talking to us. Considering his background, that shouldn't have been much of a surprise. Jim had coached for many years at Columbia and Princeton, so he had a lot of experience with players who usually aren't high on the pro scouting charts.

One of his sons, Jason, was a star quarterback at Princeton, but no NFL team would draft him. So he played in the World League and the CFL, bounced around a couple of NFL practice squads, and even went back to Princeton to coach for a year before finally hooking on with the Cowboys as a backup to Troy Aikman.

Jim has always believed that there are a lot of guys walking the street that just never get the opportunity to show what they can do.

He spoke, one on one, to every guy there, telling each of us something different. I'll never forget what he told me.

"You're going to play in this league," Jim said. "I'm not

sure if the Cowboys can use you at this point, but you are definitely worthy of being at least on a practice squad this year. If some team brings you into a camp, I think you can play in this league."

He didn't say, "Listen, son, we love you and we're going to try to get you."

I knew I wasn't the stereotypical Dallas receiver—someone who was six-foot-three or six-foot-four and could run like a deer. But he said he thought there was a spot for me somewhere in the NFL. He even promised to pass my name along to his other son, John, who was the receivers coach for the Cincinnati Bengals.

After that, my whole mentality changed. I went from being just curious about whether there might be a chance for me to make it in the NFL to saying, *I want this more than anything and I'll do whatever it takes to get on a team*. I went from being passive to aggressive about reaching the goal of signing a contract. I figured, *If this guy sees something, regardless of how true he thinks it is, someone else just might see it, too*.

It gave me a glimmer of hope. And it was the first sign of interest that Art had gotten after being rejected by any number of football people at all levels.

Sure, I've had a lot of obstacles to overcome, but I know that I'm not alone. Every year there are players—whether they're white or black, whether they're from Penn State or Hofstra—who don't get the chance to make it anywhere in pro football because they aren't drafted or don't receive a free-agent contract.

But I'll never blame the scouts for doing a bad job because they didn't have me rated. There are so many different players they're watching at so many different colleges around the country, obviously, people are going to fall through the cracks. Besides, I wasn't playing to draw attention to myself.

I was playing to win. I was playing to have fun.

I don't consider myself a poster child for every underdog there has ever been in football or sports in general. I don't want to be that. But for anybody who has ever felt they could play this game if they only got the chance, I understand what goes through their mind.

I also understand that when you get that chance, you have got to pour out every ounce of ability and desire and sweat that you have to make the most of it.

Growing up, the three people who have always mattered the most in my life—my parents and my sister, Jennifer—pushed me to give my very best. They taught me to just go out there and try not to worry about what anyone else might say about my size or the level of college ball I played or the fact I wasn't drafted. If you can look yourself in the mirror and be happy with what you see, then you know you did your best.

Throughout this long, hard, and often crazy journey to the NFL, I have made sure I look in the mirror at least once a day to see if I'm happy with the guy staring back at me.

And no matter how well I might do, I know I can always do better.

2

Trip, Fall, Bleed

Our family has always lived in New Jersey. It seems there are little pieces of Chrebet history all over the state—from Linden, where I spent my first two years on this planet; to Bloomfield, where I spent the next three years; to Garfield, where I spent thirteen years; to Wanaque, where my parents moved when I was in college; to Hackensack, where I lived during the 1997 and 1998 seasons with the Jets; to Colts Neck, where I live now.

When my sister and I were kids and we were driving around with Dad and Mom, they would always come across a part of their past.

"Look, that was our first apartment over there," my dad would say.

"Where?"

"That door."

"That door?"

Believe me, we weren't staring at the entrance to Trump Tower. At this stage of our lives, I doubt the four of us could fit inside the place, even if we were lying down, side by side.

But at least the door had a nice knocker.

Early on, my parents struggled. Wayne Sr. was a loan manager for a second-mortgage company. Mom, whose maiden name is Paulette Toth, was a secretary. She stopped working in 1971 when she was pregnant with Jen.

I came along on August 14, 1973.

Dad and Mom had a tough enough time on two salaries; going to one made things tighter. When I was really young, I remember feeling that I didn't have everything I wanted, which is pretty natural for a lot of kids to a certain extent. But we had everything we always needed, which was each other. Together, we knew we could overcome any obstacle.

There was never a shortage of love or laughter in our house. We knew that those were the main ingredients for a great life. That's how it was then when we first came into this world. And no matter how much things change or how many different directions our lives might travel, that is how it will always be.

After the second-mortgage company he worked for was sold, my father was offered a job as a collector with the new outfit. He decided that instead of collecting for someone else, he would do it for himself.

So in 1981, when I was about eight, he and my mother started their own collection agency—which they named Jenn-Way Recovery Bureau, after my sister and me—that is still going strong today. Dad sold his 1965 Corvette convertible for seventy-five hundred dollars and used the money for a deposit on office space and to buy furniture, telephones, typewriters, and whatever else was needed to get the business off the ground.

They went from having two desks in a twelve-by-fourteen room in Bloomfield to a five-person staff they have today in a much larger office in Fair Lawn. They built a small company from nothing to what it is now—even though they fired me three times along the way.

That entrepreneurial spirit tells you a lot about what kind of parents I have. They weren't afraid to take a risk to see if they could make it on their own. And they could.

My parents, like myself, have never believed that you have to settle for the backseat when there are just as many doors leading to the front.

Garfield is a small blue-collar community in North Jersey that popped up along the Passaic River, as home to the mostly Italian and Polish immigrants working in the Forstmann, New Jersey Worsted, and Samuel Hird woolen mills. It occupies just over two square miles and has a population of twenty-seven thousand.

It's only about twelve miles from New York City, but it's a world apart in terms of lifestyle. It's a scrappy, lower-middle-class town, but the loyalty and work ethic and values of the people there are strictly upper-class. It's a town where if you want something, you have to work for it—where you learn to stand up for yourself at a young age.

The Italian immigrants settled on one side of Garfield, the Polish on the other. Between them ran the only train in America that actually stopped for a red light on Monroe Street.

When I was five, we moved into a pea-green two-family house at 36 Market Street, which, our Czechoslovakian/Ukrainian heritage notwithstanding, happened to be on the Polish side of town. We lived upstairs.

The backyard was pretty much taken up by an above-ground pool that belonged to the people downstairs and that we were rarely invited to use. There wasn't much grass in the front, either. It was all driveway, then a sidewalk. My parents had planned to stay there only a year, but all of that changed after President Reagan sent interest rates climbing at the same time their bank account headed south.

The only problem I had with Garfield was that there weren't many other children for my sister and me to play with on our side of town, just elderly Polish people who weren't keen about kids playing on their lawns. Everybody who was into sports seemed to live on the other side, which was also where the Babe Ruth and Little League baseball fields, the

Boys Club and Girls Club, and the Pump House—the park that everyone played at—were located. When you're young, that's a pretty long bike ride. And there was only so much fun I could have tormenting my sister.

So I found all sorts of other ways to amuse myself . . . and get into trouble.

I guess you could say I was an energetic kid. I stuck my nose in everywhere and put myself in a lot of situations that were neither good for my health nor my parents' sanity.

I was very reckless. I pushed the limit too much—running around, slamming into things, cracking my head open, breaking bones. I was doing 360s on my Big Wheel when I was three or four. Sometimes I stayed in my seat. Sometimes I went flying.

It seemed like every time I came home, blood was flowing out of one part of my body or another.

This was a typical scene from my childhood: I would climb up on the roof of someone's garage and then jump down. I didn't care how high it was. I didn't care about the danger. My attitude was: *Let's see what happens. If I get hurt, I won't jump down again.*

I was not afraid to be a trendsetter.

Mom says I was the type of kid that, no matter where we went, I was always running way ahead of everyone else. I'll let her describe what our visits to see my grandmother in Hasbrouck Heights were like: "We wouldn't even be making the first bend and Wayne was on his way back with blood running down his face. He was always in a hurry. And he would always trip, fall."

Trip, fall, bleed. That pretty much sums up the story of my childhood.

Whenever we'd drive past Beth Israel Hospital in Passaic and see a new wing being built, my father would announce, "We paid for that." We made so many trips to the emergency room, my parents finally got a charge card that had all of their insurance information on it, which helped speed things up whenever they had to carry me in for another round of repairs.

Saying that I was accident-prone is like saying the Atlantic Ocean has a lot of water. I guess that's why there's a picture of me as a kid wearing a football helmet as I helped my father clean up leaves and branches in front of the house.

We had a white cat named Angel that I used to tease all the time. One day, Angel got even by biting into my leg so hard, you would have thought it had PURINA written on it. Then she took off for the living room to hide under the coffee table. I knew that table had sharp corners, but I never knew how sharp until I came running after the cat, stumbled, fell, and got a mouthful of one of them. I hit it hard enough that a big chunk of wood went right though my lower lip and chin. I'm not sure how many teeth I knocked out, but the next morning there was no change under my pillow, just dollar bills.

My remaining teeth were going all over the place, and I was bawling. I can't remember another time in my life when I've felt more physical pain. And this is from a 185-pound guy who, for the past four seasons, has spent Sundays on the same field as 250- and 300-pound paid assassins. Mom put me up on the counter in the kitchen, and as my face was going numb, she called an ambulance. I got my teeth fixed and ended up with twenty-one or twenty-two stitches to close the giant hole just below my lower lip. I still have the scar.

After we got home that night, I heard someone going nuts outside. I looked out the window and there was my father, on the sidewalk, with the coffee table and a hammer. He busted that thing into a million pieces. The man was actually yelling at a table while he beat the hell out of it with a hammer, sending splinters and chunks of wood all over the street. Why? Because clearly it was the table's fault that his son, his baby, had been hurt so bad—and he was going to make it pay.

The good news was that he didn't do the same thing to the relatives that had given it to my parents as an anniversary gift.

Of all of the many injuries I had to that point and of all of the ones I've had since, this was the topper. I slept with my head on my dad's chest the whole night. I couldn't eat for a while. I was drinking soup out of a straw.

But the nightmare didn't end there. Because we waited too long to have the stitches removed, the skin grew over them, so the dentist had to cut through my lip before yanking out each stitch. He didn't give me novocaine or any other painkiller. My anesthetic was my father, who sat in the dentist's chair while I sat on his lap. He had his legs hooked over mine and his arms hooked over mine. Someone else had my head.

I couldn't move. I was screaming bloody murder. Then, after pulling out half of the stitches, the dentist suddenly stopped.

"That's all I can do for now," he told my father. "You will have to bring him back another time—when he calms down—to get the rest out."

That sounded like a plan to me. But my father had absolutely no interest in putting either of us through this a second time.

"You had better take all of the stitches out right now, or you are not going to see me calm down," my father said. "You think *he* is excited? Wait until you see *me*."

The dentist took out the rest of the stitches. I screamed some more.

Did I learn my lesson? Of course not.

Remember that pool in the backyard we hardly ever got to use? I used to jump in it—from the fire escape, which was about twenty feet high. I wouldn't dive; I would do a little cannonball action and slam my ass on the bottom of the pool, which was only five feet deep. That probably wasn't healthy.

I used to ride my bike full speed toward a brick wall, then, at the last second before impact, I tried to turn and kick away from it. Sometimes I missed; other times I just bounced off and kept going; other times I ended up smashing into the wall sideways.

Why did I do it? I have no clue, but at the time it felt like the right thing to do.

My head managed to find one of the two concrete planters we had in front of our house in Bloomfield, and the result was another bloody mess. My grandma was supposed to be looking after us while my mother was in bed with a severe bronchial infection and my dad wasn't home. Mom hadn't been on her feet all day, but that all changed when she heard me screaming.

"Ma! What happened?" my mother yelled to her mother.

"He cut his head open," my grandmother said, feeling terrible that this had happened on her watch.

"Oh, my God!"

Because my grandma didn't drive, my mother, who was so dizzy that she could barely stand, was forced to get out of her sickbed and take me to the hospital. To this day, she doesn't know how she made it there without collapsing behind the wheel.

Sure enough, as Mom came staggering in with her blood-covered, screaming son, a nurse asked her, "Are you all right?"

"No, I'm not," my mother said.

So the nurse put Mom in a wheelchair, then she put me on her lap. It wasn't exactly the quality mother-son time that either of us would cherish for years to come.

When I was in first or second grade, I loved to hang with my legs over the top of a chain-link fence around the playground at School Number Four across the street from our house in Garfield. Some of the chain link was missing, so there were sections where you had only the bar going across, and it just looked so inviting to a little daredevil like me.

I would hang by the knees and hold on with my hands and just start swinging back and forth while staring at the ground. If you let go with your hands, your legs would still hold you up. But one day after letting go with my hands, I decided, for no particular reason, to straighten my legs. Sure enough, like a heat-seeking missile, with my arms at my side, I fell. I was short, so it was a good four-foot drop, and I came crashing down.

Forehead first. Right into the asphalt.

I don't remember getting up, but I do remember my sister propping me on my bike seat and pushing me home as I bled from the head and face. Jen, who is now a research reporter for *People* magazine, was supposed to be watching me while my parents visited some neighbors down the block. She was nine, only two and a half years older than me, but a whole lot wiser. It seemed like whenever we were together, Jen would inevitably have to break out the Bactine, Band-Aids, peroxide, gauze, ice bag—anything she could find to close the wounds and bring down the swelling.

When Dad and Mom walked through the door, they found me lying on the couch with a blood-soaked washcloth on my face. I don't know if I fell asleep for a second or was comatose. All I know is, as soon as my parents walked through the door, they started yelling at me. I had brought this kind of trauma onto myself so many times by then that their first instinct no longer was to ask, "Are you all right?" They felt they had to do something to put a stop to it once and for all. They would care about my injuries later.

First, they had to try to scare me into not doing crap like that anymore.

It wasn't as if my father didn't try to discipline me. It was just that I was a little wild man. Like any other kids, we got spanked and we got grounded—especially me. Dad had his own system worked out for spankings. It started out that you would get whacked on the butt five times, then each time you did something bad, the number would go up in increments of five. My total was way up there in no time at all.

But every time before he did it, whether it was five or twenty-five, he would say, "Son, this is going to hurt me more than it hurts you."

And I'd be lying across his lap, saying to myself, *If you think this is really going to hurt you that bad, you're crazy.*

Still, no amount of yelling or spanking could discourage me from pushing the limit. I don't think the word "limit" has ever been in my vocabulary.

My parents met the way most New Jersey teenagers of their generation did—while enjoying the sun, sand, and surf of the Jersey Shore. It happened in the summer of 1966 in a town called Seaside Heights.

Dad, who was from Linden, was nineteen and in the Army. After a year and a half in Berlin, he had just volunteered for service in Vietnam and was in the nineteenth day of a thirty-day furlough. Once he reached Southeast Asia, where he would be assigned to the front lines as a medic and tank driver, he wasn't supposed to be home for at least thirteen months.

Mom, who was from Hasbrouck Heights, had just graduated from high school.

As the story goes, she was alone on the beach, and my

dad spotted her on the blanket, then he followed her into the water. I guess she fell for him pretty good, because she waited for him to get back from Vietnam. Not only was there the very real chance that he wouldn't come back alive, but there was no guarantee—if he did return—that they would still be interested in each other.

Vietnam remains a very painful subject for my father. It has left him with a lot of emotional scars that can be ripped apart by something he might see or hear. I remember once when we suddenly got rid of one of our cats. Many years later, I found out that it sometimes made a gurgling noise that apparently was the exact sound that came from the throat of a man he had killed in hand-to-hand combat.

Sometimes Dad would actually wake up in the middle of the night screaming.

When we made a family trip to Washington, D.C., in 1987, my dad got within two blocks of the Vietnam Memorial Wall before he had to turn around. My mother, Jen, and I went all the way up to it, but two blocks was as close as Dad would allow himself to get.

It took almost fifteen years before he was even able to start talking with my mother in any detail about his Vietnam experience. One day they were driving down the Garden State Parkway and there was some news item on the radio that reminded him of Vietnam. He started crying, and he actually had to pull over because he couldn't see the road anymore through his tears. Right then and there, he told my mom about what he had done and what had happened—about all of the horrible things that have haunted him ever since he came back home.

I know the summary of Dad's war experience. If he wants to tell me more about it, that's fine. But I would never want to push him even close to where he would be upset or start crying. I would kill somebody else for doing that to him, to anyone else in my family, or to my girlfriend, Amy Wick.

Why would I want to be the one to do that to any of them?

Over the years, Dad has opened up a little more to me about Vietnam. The story behind the Purple Heart that he received gave me a whole new appreciation for what that honor means. In October of 1966, while stationed at a camp, he heard a call over the radio for a medic, which was a particularly dangerous position because medics were prime targets for snipers. The ones who responded to the first two calls had their legs blown off. My father responded to the third call.

While driving a tank, he came upon a ridge, then called on the radio to see whether he should turn right or left. The platoon leader told him to go left. When Dad made the turn, both tracks of his tank hit a mine and exploded. Dad was thrown thirty feet in the air; the other three men in the tank were killed. When my father hit the ground, he was a bit disoriented but not severely hurt.

Suddenly a sniper opened fire. As Dad rolled to avoid being hit, he lifted his right leg just high enough to be shot in the knee.

He has undergone at least four surgeries on the knee since, beginning with the insertion of a plastic kneecap while he was in Vietnam. After that operation, Dad was transferred to a military hospital in Japan to recuperate.

A crew from New York television station WABC, in Vietnam to interview soldiers from their viewing area, caught up with my father in Japan. I saw that black-and-white footage for the first time in 1997. It was during a special preview of an NFL Films video called *Before They Were Pros,* which aired on TNT and included segments on Brett Favre, Troy Aikman, John Elway, Marcus Allen, and yours truly. During the WABC interview, which is part of my segment, the camera pans across the ward and stops at Dad, whose right leg is in a cast. I was mesmerized. I couldn't get over how much my father, at nineteen, looked and sounded so much like me.

We even had the same haircut.

While my father was in Vietnam, he and my mother had written letters back and forth every day. But then the letters suddenly stopped. That was because my mother had no idea that my father had been shot and moved to Japan; my dad's parents didn't even know until they received a citation from the government. Because of the lack of communication, Mom and Dad each thought the other had dumped them. It took about a month before the letters from my mother finally reached Japan. Then my dad called her and they started writing again.

When my dad returned to New Jersey on Christmas Eve, 1966, my mother went to visit him. So much time had passed that she didn't even remember what he looked like.

They were engaged the following June and married a year later.

• • •

My father's wound has hampered him over the years to a certain extent. Sometimes when we played basketball, he'd jump, land the wrong way on his knee, and it would just give out. He'd be screaming.

I also know that my dad was involved in a bad accident in Vietnam in which children were killed. I don't know the complete details, but you had bullets flying all over the place that sometimes struck innocent people. Picture yourself crawling through underground tunnels, without any light, and if something moves—even if it's just a frog—you're firing first and asking questions later.

Obviously, the accident tore his heart out. At nineteen, he was a kid over there himself. And after it happened, he vowed that he would never have kids of his own.

But when he got back to the States and married my mother, he had a change of heart. He decided that bringing children into the world and taking care of them as great as he possibly could were the best ways to help make up for what happened in Vietnam.

I took Amy to see the movie *Saving Private Ryan*. As gruesome and as hectic as war seemed on film, especially in that first half hour when they're storming the beach, I'm sure it was a million times worse in real life. Right after the movie—I mean, as soon as the credits started rolling—I had to drive over to my dad's house. I really didn't need to talk with him about it, and I doubt he would have wanted to anyway.

I just needed to see him and thank him and let him know how proud I was of him.

That movie was rough on me; I can't imagine what it was like to actually fight in a war. You see that stuff on the screen, but that's Hollywood. You really don't think it could actually happen like that. It's something those of us who haven't fought in a war are never going to relate to. Some people go crazy from it. I'm just thankful that my father's mentally strong enough and that he wasn't there long enough to where it affected him in a way that he couldn't rebound from it.

To know that he was there, fighting for his country, gives me the utmost respect for him. As a tribute to my father, I have a picture hanging in my house over the television set of the Vietnam Memorial Wall with a veteran in a business suit, his briefcase at his side, crying as he touches the names of deceased soldiers.

I know I'm just a fraction of the man my father is. I mean, he's a true warrior. I might be considered a warrior on the football field, but he was a warrior in a *real* battle, where the consequences were life or death.

What my father went through gives me a great perspective on this game we play. A lot of people—players, coaches, fans, media—are so quick to compare it to war. Yes, I could get seriously injured out there, but it's just football. It's just a game. It might be a form of hand-to-hand combat where you're trying to do whatever it takes to (1) survive and (2) push the other team back.

But it definitely is not war.

I'm running down the field and I've got these maniacs chasing me. Then you have a guy out in the jungle who is literally running for his life. He has guys chasing him with guns. What we do might look like some sort of military conflict, with everybody wearing helmets and trying to knock each other's head off, but it is never going to be close to war. I have far too much respect for my father and everyone else who has actually fought in one to see it any other way.

As much as I had to overcome to get to where I am as a player, it will always dim in comparison to the things my family—and especially my father—has gone through to allow me to even have that chance.

3

Steal the Bacon

If you ask my father, he'll say that he saw the earliest signs of my natural athletic ability when I was five years old. We were playing catch with a baseball in front of the house. He threw the ball as high as he could and I caught it—with my glove behind my back.

To Dad, it was a milestone. To me, it was just a way to make playing catch a little more interesting.

The first couple of times I attempted this trick, Dad used

a hardball. After watching me take multiple conks to the head, he switched to a sponge ball. But I didn't like that. I wanted the real deal. I had never worried about my head before. Why should I start then? So I kept complaining until he went back to the hardball.

When I was seven, I used to go across the street to the front lawn of a nice yellow house on the corner. Standing on the stoop of our house, my father would throw a football through the telephone and power lines, over the street, right to where I was standing . . . and I'd catch it. We had a great time doing that.

Come to think of it, I don't know what was more impressive—me catching the ball or Dad throwing it, through those wires, right on the mark.

My most favorite game of all time, however, didn't involve a ball. It was called Steal the Bacon, which we used to play in gym class when I was in third grade. It went like this: Two teams of about twenty kids apiece would line up on opposite sides of the gym, and there would be a bowling pin in the middle, maybe twenty feet from each side. Members of each team sat on a line and would be assigned a number from one to twenty. The gym teacher would call a number, and the corresponding kid from each side had to move toward the pin.

The object was to grab the pin before the other boy or girl and get back to your home base before he or she could tag you. You could also win by tagging the other person before he or she got back to their home base. It was like a duel.

Even at a young age, I understood that there was some

strategy involved with this game and I would plot my moves every time we played. There were a lot of ways to fake out your opponent. For instance, if I intentionally came out slow, that might entice him to make a run for the pin, but then I'd suddenly turn on the speed and catch him. Or maybe, as soon as I heard my number, I'd simply explode off the line and beat the other kid to the pin and run like hell back to the line.

I know it might sound a little silly that I devoted so much thought and planning to a game as simple as Steal the Bacon. But that's just the way I have always been. I like to look at things from a lot of different angles. In any sport, you're always looking for that one little thing that will give you an edge over your opponent.

You might say the tactics in Steal the Bacon come awfully darn close to what I do when I'm one on one against a defensive back. You're just trying to make a move to get away from him and be free and clear to catch the football. Sometimes I'll come off the line slow, the DB gets lulled to sleep, then I'll make a burst, slow down again, make another burst, and—hopefully—the DB is still looking for me in one place while I'm catching the ball in another.

I also loved dodgeball. At that age, I got a real rush out of being able to smash another kid's face with a rubber ball and get away with it—or having the same done to me.

I guess the principal at our grammar school saw the same things in me that my father saw a few years earlier. During an assembly when I was in third grade, he gave me a certificate that said: MOST POTENTIAL TO BE A GREAT ATHLETE.

• • •

The first time I went to the Garfield Boys Club was with Gary Manina, a friend from grammar school, and his folks. I watched Gary play on a flag football team in the gym, and I loved everything about it. You got to throw the ball. You got to catch it. You got to chase other kids and try to grab one of the two flags attached by Velcro to the sides of the little plastic belt everyone wore. And you got to run away from the kids chasing you.

The second I got home I begged my parents to let me join so I could play, too. They were pretty quick to give in, considering that they wouldn't let me play tackle football because they didn't think it was a good idea for young boys to slam into each other and risk serious injury while their bodies were still developing.

They were particularly concerned about a certain boy whose body had gone through plenty of slamming without football.

I wound up playing all three sports the Boys Club had to offer: Pee Wee baseball, basketball (with the baskets lowered), and flag football. My favorite at that time was flag football, partly because I had a lot of success in it right away—in one of my first games, I scored nine touchdowns, still believed to be a Boys Club record—and partly because it was the first time I was around a lot of other kids on a regular basis outside of school. Up to that point, most of the things I had done in sports were usually by myself or with my sister. Now I was with twenty or thirty other kids and I was able to interact with them in an organized setting.

For the first time in my life, I was part of a team and I loved everything about it.

The positions weren't as well defined as in regular football. A lot of times I would snap to the quarterback and go out for a pass. I also played some quarterback. The gym was pretty narrow, so the more elusive you could be, the better off you were. That gave me a big edge because I was pretty elusive, having gotten so much practice running away from my parents.

You usually had four decent players on each team, but you couldn't play all four at once. And you were limited to three quarters, so you had to break up your playing time and your positions.

I played every position on the baseball team, but my best spots were center field and pitcher. My dad coached me in baseball, from Pee Wee to Little League, which made playing the game that much more enjoyable. In Pee Wee ball, the coaches pitch, so I used to stand next to him while he was pitching and field anything that came our way.

The only time it wasn't fun to have Dad as my coach was the day he benched me. It happened during the middle of a Little League game when he decided that he wanted me to play catcher. I didn't want to. I had never played there before. I didn't feel comfortable getting in a crouch. I knew that having me behind the plate didn't benefit the team, and it certainly didn't benefit me. But he put me there anyway. The first time a batter swung and missed, I was looking to see where the ball was, and it hit me right in the chest. That was it.

I was out of there.

Dad immediately yanked me from the lineup. That was the first and only time I've ever gotten benched by a coach . . . and it was by my own father.

Later on, I understood why he had to do it. If his own son wasn't going to listen to him, why should anyone else on the team? At the same time, he knew where I was coming from and actually admired the fact that I had sized up the situation and knew I had no business being at catcher.

Of course, as time goes by, I can't help but think that the *real* reason my father benched me was to get out of having to buy me a new bike. That was one of the last games of my last year of Little League, and before the season, he promised me a new bike if I hit a home run over the fence. And in that game, we were going against a pitcher that had given up a lot of home runs. My father would never admit as much, but to this day, I think he had ulterior motives for taking me out of that game.

When I was in third or fourth grade and couldn't get to the other side of town to play with kids my own age, I'd cross the street to the School Number Four playground in search of some sort of sports action, even if it meant playing by myself. You have to remember, it was just my sister and me. The family that lived below us had kids, but they were ten or fifteen years older than I was.

I can't tell you how many times I would just go across the street and shoot baskets. Or I would make up my own little games while throwing a baseball. I'd see how low I could throw it before it hit the ground, then I'd find a spot on the wall and try and hit it over and over, then I'd throw the ball as high as I could and try to catch it—sometimes behind my back.

I could amuse myself for hours that way, but it would eventually get boring. I needed some competition. Every now and then, I'd step way out of my weight class and play in pickup games with sixth, seventh, and eighth graders. They'd let me play, first, because they needed someone just to fill out a team; second, because they saw how fast I could run when my parents were chasing me.

I definitely took my lumps out there, but after a while it was a case where I showed them that I could play at their level.

Physically, I have my father's genetics. He was a super athlete, although he likes to joke that he was a legend in his own mind and that the only record he holds from his days as a five-foot-seven, 155-pound running back at Woodbridge High is breaking his collarbone four times.

My mom used to be a pretty good athlete, too. She played some basketball and volleyball in high school. She spent a lot of time bowling and playing racquetball before, I guess, my sister and I wore her down a little bit.

Jen was a very good athlete as well. She was an excellent swimmer in high school and competed in a national meet at Penn State. She also played basketball.

My sense of daring? That's from Dad all the way. For as long as I can remember, he has always had motorcycles, and I would go for rides with him all the time. When he'd come to watch me play somewhere, he'd usually be the only father to pull up on a bike. I'd see him sitting there, looking like Peter Fonda in *Easy Rider* as the motor rumbled underneath him, and I'd think, *That's a pretty cool dude.*

One time, when I was eight or nine, I took a ride with him to Allentown, Pennsylvania, to see my first college football game. We went to watch John Andrulli, one of my dad's friends, play for Muhlenberg College. I remember seeing John after the game and trying on his helmet, which almost covered me like a turtle shell. I was able to spin it all the way around my head.

It was late fall, but we didn't wear heavy coats for the two-hour ride up there because when we left, the temperature was in the sixties and it stayed that warm the whole way.

Going home was a different story.

The temperature suddenly dropped into the twenties, and we had a hundred and twenty miles of road ahead of us. Before we began our journey back to Garfield, my dad took off his jacket and put it over mine. But as soon as we started moving, I started shivering, so after a couple of miles we stopped and Dad gave me his shirt. We got going again, but after another ten minutes or so, we stopped again as Dad peeled off another layer of clothing and gave it to me. Instead of pulling his hooded sweatshirt over my head, I put my legs through the sleeves.

This little strip show kept up until—eventually—my father was down to a T-shirt and shorts. He looked like he was auditioning for a part in *The Full Monty*.

Dad was in a real dilemma because the faster he went, the

colder the wind felt, but if he slowed down, that only made the trip longer.

No matter how hard he tried to keep me warm, I was shivering and moaning every inch of the way while clinging to his waist as tight as I could. At one point, he suddenly realized there had been a long stretch where he didn't hear anything from me. Worried that maybe I had turned into an ice sculpture, he said, "What are you doing back there?"

"Crying," I said in a faint voice that was barely audible over the roar of the bike.

When we got home, Mom was ready to kill Dad for taking me along on this motorcycle-turned-sleigh ride. But she did take some pity on him because his thighs were beet-red and very sore. They would stay that way for a couple of days. It wasn't funny at the time, because we were both freezing our butts off, but when we think about it now, we can't help but start laughing. It's also another example of the extent of the sacrifice my father will make for one of his children. And it's that kind of sacrifice that keeps us the close family that we are.

Dad still has his bike. He can't ride it anymore since undergoing shoulder replacement surgery four years ago, but he has never lost that *Easy Rider* coolness.

It was Dad who gave me an up-close look at what competition and being a competitor were all about. Late in life, he became a bodybuilder, and he was so good that he went on to hold the Mr. New Jersey and Mr. East Coast titles, among others.

It all began when he turned twenty-eight. One day, while

walking down the street in Bloomfield, he saw a reflection in a store window of a guy whose looks he didn't like very much. My father headed straight for a health club and filled out a membership card.

The more time he spent working out, the more interested he became in weight lifting. Eventually, his interest turned into an obsession. It became a way of life. And, as my Dad is the first to admit, he totally disrupted our family with his diet and crazy training schedule. He drove my mother completely crazy, but we were still behind him 100 percent.

Every food in our house was dietetic. There wasn't any normal cereal, only wheat germ. There wasn't any regular milk, only skim. With Mom cooking all of this healthy bland food, is it any wonder why I didn't sprout?

I had the first pork chop of my life in November 1998 at the age of twenty-five. I was at the house of our quarterback, Vinny Testaverde, and his wife, Mitzi, cooked me one for dinner. I was so excited, I had to call my mother afterward.

"Hey, Mom, I had my first pork chop tonight," I said.

"I made you pork chops before," she said.

"Are you serious? I remember eating the same stuff every day: Pasta, chicken . . . that high-fiber cardboard that you called meatloaf."

We'd go to Friendly's and while Mom, Jen, and I ate banana splits, Dad would be sitting there with a glass of water. Some fun.

When he would be getting ready for a show, he would be on one of these low-carbohydrate diets and it would mess up his body inside. Chemically, he wasn't the same. He would always be in a bad mood. The slightest thing would set him off, which, of course, was my specialty.

About six years into my father's bodybuilding career, when I was eight, I began going with him to the gym. As usual, the first thing I looked to do was get into trouble. I'd piss my dad off somehow, and, in what seemed like a weekly ritual, I would take off like a shot down a narrow hallway leading into the men's locker room, with Pops chasing after me.

Jake Rodriguez, the racquetball pro at the health club, would take on the role of play-by-play announcer and yell, "There they go!"

I'd run through the locker room like it was a maze, cutting back and forth between lockers, darting through the shower room. My father was fast, but he didn't have a prayer of catching me. Every time, I would run down the hallway with Dad behind me and, after a couple of minutes, I would run back in the opposite direction, alone. Dad would come walking out of the locker room a short while later, exhausted. Jake would just be shaking his head and laughing.

I'm not saying that I completely understood that I was really aggravating my father. I just thought it was fun. I thought it was hysterical. That was the game to me—trying to get someone to chase me and not letting him catch me.

Sounds an awful lot like what I'm getting paid to do now, doesn't it?

One Friday when I was probably in third grade, I was hanging with Jake's daughter, Jamie, in the playroom of the health club. I was standing on a table and I told her to roll this big rubber ball across the room so I could jump on it. Sure enough, as I landed on the ball, it just shot out from under me. I went flying into the wall and came smack down on my right forearm.

I knew, right away, that I had done some serious damage to it.

Panicking, Jamie said, "I'm going to tell my daddy."

"No, no, you can't," I said.

Because I had hurt myself so many other times while fooling around, I was afraid to tell my parents or anyone else about yet another mishap. I made Jamie promise that this was going to be our little secret.

I ran into the bathroom and stuck my arm under water as cold as I could possibly get it. I held it there for like ten minutes. The rest of the day, I just held my arm close to my body at all times while trying not to be too obvious about the fact it was killing me.

My parents kind of knew something was up because I wasn't running around like a maniac as I normally did. But I made it through all day Saturday without them saying anything. On Sunday, my father and I were watching football on television. We usually wrestled during commercials, but I didn't want to that day. That's when Dad finally noticed that my arm was swollen and had turned different shades of purple and yellow.

Time to help Beth Israel Hospital build another wing.

My little stunt on the big rubber ball resulted in a broken

arm, which was put in a cast. Much to my surprise, my parents weren't all that upset with me (although I think Dad was somewhat disappointed, as was I, that I couldn't be on the field after our Boys Club Pee Wee team made the playoffs). I think they were too stunned over the fact I had walked around for almost three days with a broken arm, and no one knew about it—except me and Jamie.

Maybe that was when I developed my high threshold for pain on the football field. It was either then or the time one of my father's spankings and their incremental increases almost reached triple figures.

At first, I went to the health club with my dad just to be with him and fool around. But after a while, I began to see that if you wanted something bad enough and were willing to work for it, you could have it. I saw the muscles he built. I saw the titles he won. I saw the results of all of his hard work and sacrifice.

I would pose like my father in front of the mirror, joke around, and say things like, "Just like you, huh, Dad?"

But as I started to see what bodybuilding did to him, how obsessive it became, I kind of shied away from it. I always did sit-ups and push-ups, but I never started serious lifting until my senior year in high school, when I decided I was going to play college football.

Even now, I don't get crazy about my diet to where I'm counting calories or grams of fat. I pretty much eat what I want. It just happens that the foods I like are healthy—chicken, turkey, pasta, fruit—and I prefer drinking water and juice instead of soda. That's not to say that I won't eat an occasional Whopper at Burger King. That's not to say that I won't have a pint of Häagen-Dazs every now and then.

And if I do eat something bad, I'll just work that much harder in the gym to burn it off.

The Jets don't have me following any sort of strict diet. They only do that with the fat guys. The receivers, defensive backs, and running backs are pretty much on our own. The Jets' basic policy is if you demonstrate that you're in good shape, they'll leave you alone.

But as soon as they see that your own method doesn't work, they're going to pick your menu for you.

Being a rabid sports fan was natural around my house. Watching games on television was a ritual.

In the fall, it was the Giants and Jets on Sunday, although we were mainly Giants' fans. In the winter, it was the Knicks; never the Nets. In the spring and summer, it was the Yankees; never the Mets.

From the time I was about seven, the routine on those fall Sundays was to get home from church in time for the one o'clock kickoff, which would either be the Giants or Jets, depending on which team was supposed to play at four. Dad and I would wrestle during commercials, then, as soon as halftime came, we'd be out the front door to throw a football or baseball around.

We watched so many games over the years where the Giants would lose in the last minute; Joe Montana seemed to beat them every time that way. My father would go nuts. So would I.

"Jeez!" we'd both yell at the TV. "These guys are killing us."

We would root for the Jets, but we were die-hard Giant fans. My sister and my mom would also watch the games, with a pair of us on each couch. At times, I still find it hard to believe that now, on any Sunday in the fall, they can turn on that same TV and see me playing. It almost doesn't seem real.

I loved watching the Giants' defense in action because of great players like Harry Carson, Lawrence Taylor, George Martin, Carl Banks, Pepper Johnson, and Gary Reasons.

But the guy I paid the most attention to, of course, was the quarterback, Phil Simms. I liked him because he was always making the plays. If he stepped up to the line and the Giants needed a first down, Simms would find a way to get it for them.

I find it kind of amazing that, after all of those years of watching them as a fan, I see a lot of these guys all the time now. Carl is our director of player development. Pepper was my teammate in 1997 and on the AFC East championship squad we had in 1998.

I still appreciate those old Giant teams. I just liked the way all pro sports were played back then: basketball, baseball, football. The older players weren't playing to get to free agency and million-dollar contracts. They were playing heart and soul, blood and guts.

There are some amazing players these days, athletes with tremendous talent who can do things that those from previous decades could never dream of doing. But I try to pattern my play after the tenacity of a Dick Butkus, the gracefulness of a Gayle Sayers, and the leadership of a Joe Montana or a Phil Simms.

When you think of the Jets, you think of Joe "Willie" Namath. You think of him saying, "We're going to win the Super Bowl. I guarantee it!" I wasn't even born then, but that's what I think about. I like being a part of that tradition.

The funny thing is, growing up, I never once thought about wanting to be one of the guys I was watching on the tube. That wasn't the reason I watched. I watched because I enjoyed those moments the four of us had on a Sunday afternoon. It was such a good family thing. It was a Chrebet ritual.

As far as going to games, I got to see the Yankees more than any other team because their tickets were more affordable and available. Rooting for the Yankees just seemed like the natural thing to do as a kid growing up in northern Jersey; it still is. Even at a young age, I understood that they were the best franchise in sports.

My all-time favorite Yankee is Don Mattingly for one simple reason: He was the heart and soul of the team.

We couldn't afford season tickets to any of the New York sports teams' games, least of all the Giants'. Even if we could afford them, they were next to impossible to come by because they were all sold. Two or three times a year, whenever Dad could swing it, he'd buy two tickets from scalpers. For a couple of hundred a pop, we'd sit way up top in Giants Stadium, which was only ten minutes from our house.

On Christmas Eve, 1989, when I was sixteen, we went to see the Giants' regular season finale against the Raiders. A win would clinch the NFC East championship.

It was freezing and it felt even colder in our usual nosebleed seats. At halftime, I had about five hot dogs just to warm me up.

Then, midway through the third quarter, my father shocked me when he said, "Butch, I have to go to the car. My feet are numb."

I couldn't believe it. Biggest game of the year, the Giants are winning, and my father wants to leave?

"You can go if you want," I said. "But I'm stayin'."

And I did. I was as cold as anyone, but I wasn't about to walk out of a game like that. I stayed right to the very end, sitting there all by myself as the Giants went on to a 34–17 victory.

Everyone in the stadium was going nuts, celebrating the fact the Giants had won their second division title in four seasons. The place was louder than I had ever heard it before. And I have never forgotten what that accomplishment meant to the fans. It was in the back of my mind on December 19, 1998, the day we beat the Buffalo Bills on the road to clinch the AFC East and give the Jets their first division championship since 1969, the last year of the American Football League.

I had a real understanding, from a fan's point of view, of how long the Jets' faithful had been waiting for that moment.

As we got later and later into the season and we got closer and closer to clinching the division, the fans were louder with each game. I felt the same way nine years earlier, rooting for my team.

Sitting by myself in the upper deck of Giants Stadium that day, I saw Harry Carson and Pepper Johnson dump Gatorade on their head coach, Bill Parcells. Nine years later, standing on the sidelines in Orchard Park, New York, I was teaming up with Bobby Hamilton to dump Gatorade on our head coach, Bill Parcells.

There were 70,306 people in the stands the day I saw the Giants win that division crown. After the final gun sounded, there were 70,305—excluding my father.

When I came down to the car, I couldn't believe what I found. There was Dad, sitting in the front seat with his jacket off, sweaters off, and shoes off. He had cranked the heater so high it must have been nine hundred degrees. And as he sat there, listening to the game on the radio and taking a steam bath, he had become a little drowsy. Everyone around him is acting like it's New Year's Eve in Times Square, and he's half-asleep.

I had wanted to tell him all about the great quarter and a half he had missed, but I was laughing too hard to speak.

I still can't believe he left something like that. I've never let him live it down.

I was so accident-prone as a kid, I had to wear a football helmet just to help with yard work. *(Author's collection)*

Yeah, I know I was a cute little bunny. Sleeping Beauty is my sister, Jen. With Halloween costumes like that, you knew we were going to clean up big time on candy. *(Author's collection)*

Taking yet another tumble. *(Author's collection)*

No one's going to mess with this dynamic father-son duo. *(Author's collection)*

How could a sweet, innocent face like this ever get into any trouble? *(Author's collection)*

I got an early start on my lunch-pail work ethic. *(Author's collection)*

There was no lightbulb, but I didn't take any chances as I removed the shade on the lamp of the helmet of my favorite team growing up. *(Author's collection)*

Check out Dad's hair when he brought my sister and me to Bat Day at Yankee Stadium. *(Author's collection)*

My father snapped this shot as I was being hauled away because of dehydration . . . just before he joined me in the ambulance with a broken wrist. (*Author's collection*)

Wearing lucky number 7 for the Garfield Boilermakers.
(*Author's collection*)

This was one leadoff hitter who was always looking to swing away.
(Author's collection)

On Graduation Day at Garfield with Grandma, the sweetest, kindest, most generous person I have ever known . . . and a continuing source of inspiration.
(Author's collection)

Putting on a move after the catch while at Hofstra. *(Photo courtesy of Hofstra Athletic Communications)*

Covered with Maine mud in my junior year as my sister, Jen, watches from a safe distance. *(Author's collection)*

Finding the end zone. *(Brian M. Ballweg)*

We're number one! *(Author's collection)*

Giving a serious pose for my senior photograph in college. *(Author's collection)*

That's Luke, worn out after one of our training sessions before I reported to my first training camp with the Jets. *(Author's collection)*

Posing with the 1994 Iron Mike Award with Hofstra president Dr. James M. Shuart and our great quarterback Carlos Garay, who won the Hofstra Pride Club Senior Recognition Award. *(Jim Sheehan)*

4

"Just Run Between Joe and Dave"

My parents didn't think football was my calling, which was why they were so reluctant to sign the permission slip when I decided to go out for Garfield High's varsity team as a sophomore.

Who could blame them? I was really small, only five-foot-three. I was really skinny; I couldn't have weighed more than 130 pounds.

Those dimensions might have been OK for the sports I

played as a freshman, basketball and baseball, but football? I had to be joking, right?

Wrong.

Dad signed the permission, although he would later admit that he had only done so because he figured I would quit before I ever actually set foot on the field for a game.

The year before I had thought about going out for the freshman team, but I couldn't because in early August I had broken yet another bone in my body—this time my ankle—and it wasn't completely healed.

The injury occurred about five minutes into my first practice at a weeklong summer basketball camp in Lawrenceville, New Jersey. My dad had just dropped me off and was making the two-hour drive back to Garfield. Mom and Jen were spending the week at Ocean Beach with my Uncle Al, who has since passed away, and his family. Jen's boyfriend was there, too, for what they had planned to be a nice, relaxing vacation.

After Dad got home, I gave him a call.

"I have a problem," I said.

Right away, my father suspected the worst. He had gotten a lot of practice through so many other dealings with me over the years.

"Wayne, please tell me that you forgot your wallet. Please tell me you don't have your extra pair of sneakers. Tell me anything but what I think you're going to tell me."

"Sorry, Dad . . ."

I proceeded to explain that as I was going up for a rebound, I landed on the side of someone's foot and my right ankle just buckled and snapped.

My father took a deep breath and said, "I'm on my way."

The next day, after yet another visit to the hospital, Dad drove me down to Ocean Beach. Because I couldn't get sand inside my cast, he put me over his shoulder like a sack of potatoes, carried me across the beach, laid me down on the blanket next to my mother, and said, "He's all yours."

Then he went back to work.

After their initial shock wore off, it didn't take long before Mom and Jen were ready to drown me. I was absolutely miserable. Here it was, summer and not only couldn't I do the thing I was supposed to be doing at the time—playing basketball—but I couldn't even have any fun at the Shore, either.

So I made it my mission the rest of that week to make everyone else as miserable as I was, which isn't very difficult when you're sitting in a wheelchair ("Hey, it isn't fair that you guys get to go to the Boardwalk and I have to stay here! Take me with you! Push me along! It isn't fair!!!") or spending a week in a small overstuffed cottage.

A short while later, we took a family trip to Washington, D.C. I was still in the wheelchair—and desperate to find some amusement. The sun was blazing, the temperature had to have been nearly a hundred degrees. But like the Griswalds, we were determined to see all of the sights.

One day as we headed up the hill to the Washington Monument, my father couldn't figure out why he was struggling so much to push me—especially with all of the weight lifting he had done through the years.

When we finally got to the top, I kind of gave him a little

wiseass smile and, pretending to be concerned, I said, "Gee, Dad, you having a tough time?"

"Yeah, Butch," my father said. "I don't know what's wrong with me."

"Well, maybe it wouldn't have been so hard if I didn't have the brake on the whole time."

I'm fortunate that he had a good enough sense of humor not to just turn that wheelchair around and send it flying down the hill into traffic. I definitely had it coming.

That fall I watched some of the varsity football games at Garfield and thought, *Wow, that looks like fun.* Unlike freshman games, which were played during the week, varsity games were on Saturday and attracted much larger crowds. A lot of girls were in the stands, which I thought was especially important.

The head coach, Ed "Huff" Kotwica, had coached my sister in basketball. He also knew my parents, so I figured, *If nothing else, he might patronize me and give me a shot.*

When he first saw how small I was, however, it was all he could do not to burst out laughing. I think he might have thought there was something wrong with my eyes—that maybe I couldn't see how much bigger than me the other guys going out for the team were.

I saw them. I can honestly say I never gave their size, or mine, a second thought.

Huff granted what I'm sure he viewed as my "death" wish. But he had no idea where to play me. I had no idea where I should play, either. The only thing I did know was what number I wanted: 7, my lucky number. If nothing else, I figured I would at least have *that* going for me.

Finally, Huff decided to put me at wide receiver, although I seriously doubt he pictured me being able to do anything more than fit into a uniform. And he probably wasn't too sure about that.

No matter where I played, I faced an obstacle that I considered more challenging than my size: I really didn't know very much about football. Baseball? No problem. I knew it front to back. Basketball? A breeze. Football just seemed to tie my brain in knots.

Even after playing flag football until fifth grade and playground football every chance I got, even after all of those years of watching the Giants and Jets on television, I really didn't know what the game was all about. I didn't understand each position or what everybody's responsibilities were. I didn't know how plays were supposed to be run. I didn't know any of the strategy involved.

When practice first started, I was all messed up, running the wrong plays and facing the wrong direction. For that reason, my father's prediction almost came true. I started thinking that maybe he and my mother were right—maybe football wasn't for me. It's not that I was feeling any sense of failure or that it was something I thought I was physically incapable of doing. It's just that I didn't know what to do, and it became frustrating. It was like everyone around me was speaking a foreign language and I was being left out of the conversation.

It went from getting in the huddle in flag football or a

schoolyard game and saying, "I'm going to run deep," or "I'm going to go ten yards and break left," to "Forty-two Power Pass" or whatever it was called. I had never dealt with a numbering system like that before, and it confused me to the point where I was mixing up the plays.

After taking some time to think things over, I decided it would be better to try to stick it out rather than quit. The idea of quitting seemed to bother me a lot more than struggling to grasp the finer points of football.

I never wanted to be known as a quitter in anything I did.

Little by little, the situation in practice began to improve. Sometimes I still didn't know what I was doing, but I could always catch the ball. And the more catches I made, the more plays I would get in practice.

Before I knew it, it was the day before our season opener and we were having a pep rally. The whole school was packed in our dungeonlike gym to make some noise for the Garfield Boilermakers. At this point, I was just happy that I made the team, that I was wearing a uniform, that I was part of something filled with so much energy and excitement.

With all of these kids yelling and screaming and stomping their feet, the public address announcer began to introduce the starting lineup. I was getting ready to clap for the first of my teammates whose name would be called when, all of a sudden, I heard something I never expected to hear in a million years: "At flanker . . . number seven . . . Wayne Chrebet!"

I was literally in midclap, with my hands about an inch apart and my mouth hanging open in shock. The next thing I knew, I was running out to all of these cheers, praying every step of the way that I didn't slip and fall because we were all in our socks (to avoid scuffing the gym floor) and because Accident was my middle name.

It was one of the greatest feelings I've ever had because, for one thing, it was the first time I saw that there was a payoff for my hard work and willingness to hang in there and, for another, I didn't fall during the introduction.

That first season I had to play free safety on the scout team in practice. The scout team's role is to help the starting offense and defense get ready for the game by simulating the other team's plays. I was having a hard enough time getting down my assignments as a receiver, so throwing free safety duties into the mix put a real overload on my brain. I tried to make it simple by watching which direction the strong safety went after we broke the huddle. If he went left, I knew I had to go right, and vice versa.

The only time my size might have caused a little bit of a problem was during those scout team periods when I had to face Chuck Danys, our beast of a running back. Compared to most everyone else on the team, Chuck was a monster, about five-foot-nine and 185 pounds. He was one of the better athletes in the school and a really good wrestler. He would pin guys in ten seconds—just grab them and slam them to the mat. He would charge at his opponents, they would practically crap their pants on the spot, and the dungeon would go nuts.

He was tough. He was serious. He was out there to kill someone. And I'm supposed to tackle this guy in practice?

Get real.

The typical scene went something like this: Chuck would take the handoff, I'd move in front of him, he'd run me over. It happened, day in and day out, like a ritual. I'm talking about literally running me over, literally stepping on my body. I didn't even get a hand on him, but I stayed in there, figuring that I would get him down eventually. I thought, *If I at least fall in front of him often enough, there might be one time when I'll trip him up.*

But all I did was give the guy a carpet, with lucky number 7 on it, to clean his cleats as he chugged downfield.

To this day, I don't know how I ended up starting on the football team that first year. Most of my pass routes were a mystery to me, as were almost all of the other positions, about 90 percent of our plays, and the signals used to call them. I relied more on my ability to memorize where I was supposed to line up and run than on my actual understanding of the offense.

This sort of thing went on for two more seasons. In my senior year, we had a play where I would line up in the slot, like a wingback, and I would take the ball on a reverse. Huff would say, "Go between the guard and the tackle."

I had no clue what he was talking about. I knew the receivers and the quarterback and the running backs, but I didn't understand who was the guard and who was the tackle.

Finally I said, "I don't know who are you talking about."

So Huff said, "Just run between Joe and Dave."

This was my third season of playing organized football, and it was midway through the year before I figured out where the guard and tackle lined up.

At the end of my junior year and into my senior year, I started at free safety, as well as at receiver. By that point, I finally had a good grasp of the offense, but defense was a different story. I still didn't always know where I was supposed to line up as a free safety. And because I wasn't always sure which man I was supposed to cover on pass plays, I hoped the other team would run the ball.

I knew, whatever hole that back came through, all I had to do was run up as fast as I could and slam my face right into him. There was no form tackling, no wrapping the guy up with my arms. I was just sticking my head in there and giving the best pop I could. I had to make those hits count because if I didn't knock the guy down that way, he probably was going to keep on running all the way to the end zone.

I liked to tackle as much as I liked catching passes, maybe more. That's one of the great things about football: You can hit somebody and not get suspended from school or sent to jail. I wasn't trying to kill anyone. And at five-foot-eight and 155 pounds, it wasn't much of a possibility.

I just loved to sit back there and try to lay a lick on people.

Generally, I did all right in pass coverage because if someone ran behind me, I was fast enough to catch up to him. Besides, no quarterbacks in our league had a super arm. I ended up with only one career interception, but it did come at a great time—my last game against Lodi, our biggest rival. Garfield–

Lodi games were known as "The Battle of Harrison Ave.," because that was the street that separated the two communities.

Looking back, the struggles I had with all of the X's and O's helped me to become the student of the game that I am today. If I'm going to do something, I'm going to do it right. So I started studying the plays more and more, just trying to understand all of the strategies and the small things that can give you an edge on the field.

I realize this early lack of knowledge about the game doesn't say a whole lot for the coaching I received, but it wasn't the coaches' fault. I just never asked any questions. I wouldn't allow myself to say, "Listen, I really don't know what I'm doing."

It was a pride thing. I just thought I would pick it up as I went along.

I actually had a lot of respect for our coaches, especially Huff, who was a defensive tackle on Garfield's last state championship football team in 1965. He helped me a lot. Not so much with the X's and O's, but just the emotional part of it. He could see when I was confused or down on myself, and he would help get me through it.

Every Sunday during the season, I would go over his house and the two of us would watch the film of the previous day's game, with a critical eye on every aspect of my performance. The rest of the team saw it in school a day or two later.

You trusted what Huff said because he had a great understanding of football and life in general. He also had a great sense of humor. He would constantly bust our chops with wisecracks, and we would go right back at him while still maintaining respect. He liked to call me "Mush," because he said I spoke so fast as a kid that I tended to mush all my words together. When he came into the huddle, we told him his breath smelled like kielbasa.

Huff gave us the freedom to cross the line, to be ourselves, without losing control of the team. He made football fun, which was a big reason that I developed such a great love for the game.

Of course, that didn't mean we were always best buddies. I had my share of run-ins with Huff, especially in my senior year. I remember one game when I had a hundred and fifty yards receiving in the first half. Our quarterback, Julio Collazo, and I had connected on eighty- and seventy-yard touchdowns. We were on our way to being named coplayers of the week in our league.

Then, in the second half, Huff just stopped throwing the ball and kept it on the ground for the rest of the game.

I complained so much that under my picture in Garfield's Class of 1990 yearbook, it says: "Hey, Huff, what about the second half?" At the time, I just thought he was trying to hold us back. But through the years, I came to realize that he needed to give other players on our team a chance to succeed on the field and that he didn't want to rub it in the other team's face.

It was a lesson about sportsmanship that I have never forgotten.

Huff left most of the disciplining to his assistant coaches,

Charlie Rigoliosi and Steve Mucha (who is now Garfield's head coach). You did not want to mess with those guys. So it was a good combination, with Huff keeping things light and the assistants staying on our butts.

I spent most of my time in practice with Charlie Riggs because he coached receivers and defensive backs. He also had been my freshman baseball coach and was my teacher for computer science, which is one of my favorite subjects. He was the one that taught me about hand positioning to catch the ball: If the pass is low or too far to the outside, keep your thumbs out; if it's right at you or you're going high for it, thumbs in. Just the fundamentals.

Riggs was a small fiery kind of guy, very energetic. He would tell you what you were doing wrong, but he wouldn't degrade you. I liked the fact that he would get in there and physically show you how to do something.

All of those coaches are great guys and people I still keep in touch with to this day. Huff was there from the start and has been there ever since, even after his retirement following my senior season. He regularly attended my games at Hofstra, and still comes to my games with the Jets. Every year before I went back to college training camp, I would stop by his house. We would sit in his backyard, drink some lemonade, and just talk.

He is part of the Chrebet family. He is not someone who asked to be a part of our family or needs to be or needs any kind of pat on the back because he was my high school coach. Huff has just always been there. He is a genuine person, someone I can call on at any time.

And when we don't get to talk to each other, he will e-mail me after every game, saying things like: YOU NEVER CEASE TO AMAZE ME.

That means a lot, because Huff is not someone who hands out compliments for the heck of it.

Garfield High might have been small—there were only about a hundred and seventy-five kids in our graduating class—but we always had a tremendous amount of pride.

Garfield still calls itself the City of Champions because the 1939 Boilermakers traveled to the Orange Bowl on Christmas night and beat Miami High, 16–13, for what was considered the mythical national championship of scholastic football. It extended Garfield's winning streak to twenty-one and ended Miami's at eighteen.

Sixty years later, and you can find people around town who will tell you all about how quarterback Bennie Babula, in the only field-goal attempt of his high school career, kicked the winning points from twenty yards with less than four minutes to play.

Right after he made the sign of the cross in the middle of the field.

I got to meet Bennie, who had all kinds of great stories from that team. From what I've heard, the head coach, the late Art Argauer, used some pretty offbeat tactics to motivate his players. Once, when they were getting ready to play Bloomfield, he chased everyone but the regulars out of the locker room. Then he said, "I'm going to give you guys a pill which you can't tell anyone about. It'll make tigers out of you. After you take this, I want you to make sure you don't hit anyone too hard because you may hurt them."

Those *pills* turned out to be candy. But the players apparently bought into their "magic" because they held Bloomfield to minus yardage on the way to an 18–0 win.

We had some good athletes when I was at Garfield High, but because it was such a small school, guys needed to play just about every sport in order for us to have an athletic program. It also helped if you could play different positions in the same sport, which many of us did.

On the football team, I was part of a nucleus of about five or six guys that never left the field. In my senior year, I played wingback, free safety, a little cornerback, and punter. I returned kickoffs—I even took one back for a touchdown—and punts. I covered kickoffs and punts. I blocked on extra points. And I held for the placekicker, which was a position Julio filled when he wasn't playing quarterback . . . or returning kicks.

I had my biggest year on offense as a senior, catching twenty-six passes for five hundred-plus yards and eight touchdowns. Chuckie Hawthorne, my good friend and fellow receiver, was the only other person on the team to catch more than a handful of passes.

We knew we didn't have the numbers to ever go undefeated. In my three seasons, our best record was maybe a game or two above .500. But whatever we didn't accomplish in terms of victories, we made up for in toughness. We took pride in the fact we were usually able to knock a couple of our opponents' players out of the game. Teams would beat us and we kind of understood that that would happen sometimes. But we always left them with some bumps and bruises to remember us by.

We could be just plain nasty out there.

Most of the guys who played football also wrestled during the winter—I think I was the only one who played basketball—and they loved to mix it up on the field. We played an aggressive, physical style. Nobody would back down.

To this day, I play football the way I learned it from teammates like Chuck Danys, Eric Garcia, Julio Collazo, and Dave Takach. Hit anything that moves. Take no prisoners. If I played on a team with a bunch of powder puffs, I might be a powder puff. But then I'm pretty sure I wouldn't be writing about my journey to the NFL. This trip would have ended a long time ago.

Surprisingly, most of our games at Garfield didn't turn into big brawls. In fact, in my three years, it only happened once—during the final game of my junior season.

Nonetheless, it is a game I'll never forget.

We had just lost at Waldwick High, where Dave Fiore, a former teammate of mine at Hofstra who would eventually play for the San Francisco 49ers as an offensive tackle, was playing at the time. It was one of those games that left a lot of sore feelings. There were some questionable calls by the officials and some questionable hits from both sides.

Someone from Waldwick delivered a cheap shot to our

smallest player, a receiver called Juney, and the rest of us took offense to that. Juney stood only about five-foot-two, but he was as tough as nails. He was a lightweight wrestler who wouldn't back down from anyone. So during the course of our retaliation, little fights broke out on the field, but they stopped almost as soon as they began.

However, a serious brawl erupted after the game when players from both teams were shaking hands. It was just mayhem.

We were all in there trying to hold our own. The problem was, you didn't know where the next punch was coming from. Like a numb nut, I had already taken off my pads and helmet, which put me at a disadvantage from the start.

Dad, along with other parents and adults from both schools, came running onto the field to get all of the players separated.

"Are you all right?" he asked.

"Yes, I'm fine," I said. "No big deal."

Finally the fight ended and everything was calm. Dad was with my mom, my grandma, my uncle, and a couple of my cousins, and they were going to head for the car while I headed for the team bus.

"Where's your car?" I asked my father.

He pointed to where it was, and I could see trouble brewing. To get to the car, he would have to walk past a lot of Waldwick people who were still mad about what had just happened. I knew my father wasn't too happy, either. Between worrying about me and thinking about the officials, he was working with a pretty short fuse.

"Dad, why don't you just go around that way?" I said, pointing to where he could get to his car while avoiding any potential trouble.

Of course, he ignored me and just kept walking straight ahead. I got on the bus.

Sure enough, as I would later find out, some guy started talking crap to my father. My father, who was forty-two at the time, stopped, turned, and quietly said, "Look, I'm not one for words. If you've got something to do, do it."

The guy, who was almost twenty years younger, came right after him. Realizing that he owned his own business and didn't want to put it in jeopardy, Dad decided to swing at the guy's chest, rather than at his mouth.

He put him on the ground with one punch.

Then two of the guy's friends jumped on top of my father. My mother grabbed one of them by the hair and started kicking him in an effort to get him away from Dad.

As all of this was going on, I watched from the bus with my jaw dropped. I couldn't believe it. But as much as I hated for something like that to happen, part of me couldn't help but be proud of the fact that my parents were sticking up for themselves and for each other.

Not that that mattered to the police, who arrested my father and the first guy he started fighting with for creating a public disturbance. When I got home, all I could say to my father was, "What's wrong with you, dude?"

For his court appearance, my dad showed up wearing his usual nice suit jacket and a tie, looking very businesslike. The other guy showed up in a black T-shirt he had gotten at some rock concert. The judge first asked the other guy for his name, age, and hometown. When he mentioned he was from Clifton, Dad said, "Wait a second. This was a Waldwick–Garfield game. What were you doing there?"

"I just got so excited from all of the action," he said. "I had to join in."

After Dad revealed his age, the judge put his hand over the microphone, leaned forward, and said, "Mr. Chrebet, what the hell happened?"

"Judge, please," my father said. "Do whatever you have to do to me. I'll pay whatever fine I have to pay. Just let me get out of here."

The fine was four hundred and forty dollars, and if he behaved himself for six months—which he managed to do—his record would be clean.

Not long after that, my parents were at the school for a basketball game. As soon as they walked in, the theme from *Rocky* began blaring over the loudspeakers. My father smiled sheepishly as one of the teachers jokingly walked past him with a timid look and said, "Don't hit me! Don't hit me!"

He and my mother were so embarrassed.

I'd love to say that was the last time my father wound up having something crazy happen to him at one of my football games. It wasn't.

And the next crazy incident involving Dad was the very next game we played—the first one of my senior year, against Hawthorne.

I have never been much for having a lot to eat or drink the day of a game, and it usually isn't a problem. Except for this day. It was really hot and, for the first time in my life, my legs started cramping. I tried to get the cramps rubbed out, but as I would learn, dehydration is the kind of thing that once it hits you, you can't fight it. You need time—and in severe cases an IV—to recover.

But I went out there for another play, which turned out to be a reverse to me. As I was getting tackled, my whole body tensed up: my calves, my hamstrings, my arms . . . every-thing cramped up at once. I had no idea what was happening to me. I was just screaming, rolling around on the field in ag-ony.

My father was standing behind the fence that sur-rounded the field. He didn't want to take the time to walk around to the gate, so he jumped over. In doing so, his hands slipped off and he went crashing to the ground, landing hard on his wrist. He knew right away that it was badly broken. He just didn't want everyone else to know, least of all the cheer-leaders who were looking down at him, wondering what the heck was going on.

For a second, Dad wondered if he should just stay on his back and wait for a stretcher or just pop back up and act like nothing happened. As usual, the old Chrebet pride took over, and, even though his wrist was flopping all over the place and he was in serious pain, he got right back on his feet and headed to the bench, where I was being tended to.

The doctor told my father that I was pretty badly dehy-drated and that I would have to go to the hospital for an IV.

71

"Well, you might want to take a look at me, too," Dad said. "I think I've broken my wrist."

For my father to even say something like that, I knew that he must have done some major damage to himself. Sure enough, after I was helped into the ambulance, in came my dad, his wrist broken in two places. And off we went, side by side, to the hospital. I wound up getting a couple of bags of fluid; Dad wound up getting a cast.

I wonder if the people at the hospital thought we were looking for one of those buy-one-get-one-free deals?

The funny thing is, my mother was videotaping the entire time, but she had the camera pointed in another direction. So even though you don't actually see my father take his fall, you do hear the thud of him hitting the ground . . . then you hear the whole crowd and the cheerleaders react by taking a deep breath in unison, "HUUUH!"

I'd love to say that *that* was the last time my father wound up having something crazy happen to him at one of my football games.

But the second week of the season brought a whole new Chrebet family adventure.

The weather was a little cooler than it was in the first game, so Dad was wearing a loose-fitting sweatshirt. As he leaned against the fence, with a cast on his wrist, a bee found just enough room to fly up his sweatshirt and start stinging the living heck out of him.

After what he had been through, the last thing in the world my father wanted to do was cause another commotion by going nuts and ripping his shirt off, which I'm sure he felt like doing. So he just stood there, holding the fence and gritting his teeth, as the bee continued to sting him for a while before it finally flew away.

Until my father's incredible three-game stretch, I never knew that being a spectator was so hazardous to your health.

5

The Ultimate
Team Sport

Even after two years of varsity football, the sport that my father thought was going to give me the best chance at a college scholarship was basketball.

I'll admit, I was probably better at basketball than football in high school. And basketball definitely was my favorite sport to play. It still is.

Anytime someone feels the need to validate my credentials as an NFL player, one of the first things you hear about is the fact that, despite being five-foot-ten, I can dunk a basketball. I've been able to do that since my sophomore year of college. I'm pretty proud of it, although I don't think I will ever entertain any thoughts of trying to make an NBA roster.

I practically lived under the basket at the School Number Four playground across the street from our house. I was there day and night, from grade school to high school, year-round. I would be there even if it were snowing. That's the beauty of shooting baskets. It's something you can always do, regardless if anyone else is around.

Across from School Number Four was Our Lady of Sorrows Church. Two nights a week, when Bingo was being played there, the playground was filled with cars, leaving us little or no room for basketball. We asked a cop who directed traffic if he would keep just enough cars off the playground to leave about a third of the court open so we could still try our three-pointers. He usually did.

Of course, even if cars were under the basket, that never stopped us from taking shots. We did our best to protect the cars, but I can't lie. Occasionally, the ball hit a windshield or two . . . or three.

When I didn't play basketball outside, I played it inside, using the basket in my bedroom. Not a Nerf basket, but a regulation metal hoop, on a small backboard attached to a short pole, that I set up against a wall. The ball I used was a little smaller than regulation—the kind you can get down at the Boardwalk—but it was perfect for my little bedroom. Besides, I wasn't allowed to dribble in the house; I had to make believe.

What I could do was lay on my back and just shoot the ball up from the floor all day, seeing how many baskets I could make in a row. It was a fairly short shot, compared to what you did on a court, but it still was good practice. Being the kind of kid that I was, I had plenty of opportunity to hone my shooting because I spent a lot of time in my room—and not by choice.

I have always loved the skill and strategy involved in basketball. I have always loved the speed of the game.

Basketball is the ultimate team sport, with five people working within the same system. There is nothing like being in a big game, on any level, and coming down to make a big basket—then turning around to see four buddies behind you cheering you on.

I was on a basketball team with the same three kids from third grade through high school. There was Chris Annibal (who is still one of my best friends in the world), John Sangis, and Ty McCullough. You knew what the other guy was going to do on the court before he did it.

We had a run-and-gun team at Garfield. I was the point guard, which made me the coach on the floor. I had to call the plays, I had to run the offense and the defense. I loved to drive and push the ball up the court. I loved to shoot, too, but the most fun for me was just driving up and down the floor, trying to create stuff.

I liked trying to make that unbelievable pass—the no-look bounce, the behind-the-back—or just a plain old chest pass to Sangis, who was always outside the three-point arc. And I loved driving the lane. The problem was, once I got going, I usually couldn't stop.

I probably have the school record for most charges in a career.

I was a good shooter. I came within about forty points of having a thousand for my high school career. The main reason I didn't hit the thousand-point mark was because we had such a good team in my senior year. We had a 21–5 record, and because we would be way ahead of most teams by halftime, our coach would have the starters on the bench the entire second half.

We weren't too happy about it, but there wasn't a whole lot any of us could do—except try and score as many points as we could in those first thirty minutes.

In all, we had three guys who could have potentially scored a thousand in our careers, and Ty, who had eleven hundred and fifty, a school record. I had nine hundred and sixty, John had nine hundred and forty, and Chris had nine hundred.

Defense was probably my favorite end of the game, though. And I wasn't any less aggressive there. I picked up a lot of fouls because I would not concede a basket. If someone was on a breakaway and I was in the lane, I would get a piece of him. I wasn't a dirty player, but you weren't going to get anything for free from me.

It was just the principle of it.

Amazingly, I fouled out of very few games. I knew when

to back off, especially later on in my career when I had a better understanding of how important it was to stay in the game. Besides, my parents went through a lot of trouble to make sure that, when Jen and I were playing varsity basketball on the same day, at least one of them was at our games. The rule they had was that Dad went to all of the away games, no matter who was playing, and Mom was at all of the ones at home.

One of my most memorable games was in my senior year, in the state semifinals at Harrison High School. Ray Lucas, a backup quarterback that the Jets picked up in 1997, was on that team. We lost, but Ray's school cheated.

Harrison was notorious for turning up the heat of its gym to about ninety-five degrees and sweating the other team out. We were a run-and-gun team in good shape, but after five minutes in that place, we couldn't breathe. It was horrible. We were dying, dripping with sweat. People in the stands were sweating like they were in a sauna. In fact, after the game, we ended up jumping in Harrison's pool with our uniforms on; that's how unbearably hot it was.

When Ray first joined the Jets, I walked up to him and said, "I remember you; you cheated."

He started laughing, but he admitted, "Yeah, we used to turn that heat up on teams."

My father was so convinced I could at least get a basketball scholarship from a small college, he wanted me to give up my senior year of football to avoid risking an injury that might keep me from playing hoops.

"That's enough, Butch," Dad said. "You've had your fun.

You played two years of football and got it out of your system. Now you can focus all of your attention on basketball."

How serious was he about this? Serious enough to threaten not to sign the permission form for football.

As I said, I loved basketball, but at that point in my life, I wasn't thinking about what sport was going to be my ticket to college. The only thing I knew was that I had a lot of fun playing three sports in high school—football, basketball, and baseball—and I wasn't about to give up one for the sake of another. To me, that would be like quitting. I have always believed that you finish what you start, and I wasn't finished with football.

Not yet. Not for at least one more season.

I pleaded with my father to see it my way.

"Dad, this is going to be my last year of playing football, and I'll probably never get to play it again," I said. "I have my friends on the team . . . I think I can have a big year catching the ball . . . Just let me finish."

Much to his dismay, I eventually convinced him to sign the permission form one last time. Thank God for that.

Who knows what I'd be doing now if he didn't?

I was a pretty good baseball player, although my talents were never going to attract any scholarship offers or a contract from the Yankees.

My batting average was good. I hit .400 in my senior year, but not because I had all clean solid hits. It was because I would beat out a lot of stuff. I was a leadoff hitter, but I might have walked once in my senior year. I had the mind-set that when I was up there, I was swinging three times. I wasn't going to swing at the ones over my head, but if I was up there, I was getting my money's worth.

As dangerous as I was in every other facet of my life, it shouldn't come as any surprise that I managed to wreak a little havoc with a baseball bat. I was the first guy up for batting practice one day, and the first pitch the head coach, Butch Wiatrak, threw, I swung hard and hit a screamer right back at him. He tried to jump, but it was too late. The ball broke his ankle. He wound up in a cast for a while, so Charlie Riggs had to come up from the freshman team to help him out.

I wasn't any less aggressive on the bases. Anytime I got on first, I was stealing, no matter what. I didn't care if the pitcher threw it over there; I was going. And I usually made it to second.

I pitched and played third base on our freshman team, which did really well. My pitching record was 5–1.

We also had a very strong varsity team, on which I began playing third before being permanently moved to center field, my favorite position.

The defensive part of baseball has always been the most fun for me. I could shag fly balls all day. I just loved running around and diving to make catches all over the place. The harder the catch, the better I liked it. I didn't like the ones that were hit right at me. I loved the ones that were hit right or left or over my shoulder.

In a lot of ways, they're the same type of catches I make

today, minus the glove and the headhunter looking to plant his helmet between the "8" and the "0" on my jersey.

Probably the best catch I ever made, in baseball or football, came in a state playoff baseball game against Lenape Valley during my senior year. Lenape is a much bigger school than Garfield, with a roster loaded with big strong farm kids. Our tallest guy was six-foot-one; they had six-foot-five trees on their team. And one of them launched a rocket. Right from the ping of the aluminum bat, I knew this thing was going deep and I just turned my back to home plate and ran. I didn't even hesitate. There were no fences at Garfield, so I would play shallow and trust my speed that I could get to anything.

When I finally looked over my shoulder, that ball was still sailing. So I decided to just lunge, with my back to home plate, diving straight for it like Jim Edmonds of the Anaheim Angels. I had my glove, which was on my left hand, outstretched and my right hand behind the glove. The ball went right into the mitt, and then I fell, hanging on to the ball. It was actually like a football catch.

If I wasn't playing football and could only do one thing in sports, I would shag fly balls. I could do that all day, every day. That just beats all!

Why? Just because it's something that I have done my whole life. I have caught baseballs every conceivable way. I love catching them behind my back. I love catching them over the shoulder.

I love making the Rickey Henderson snap catch, although I'd never do that in a game because I wasn't a hot-dog.

Just as in football and basketball, I was all-league and all-county for baseball. I wasn't one of the guys who I thought were good enough to have played professionally if they ever got the chance—guys like John Sangis and the Montelbano twins, Kevin and Keith.

But making the pros wasn't the reason I played the game. All I ever wanted out of baseball was the same thing I wanted out of football and basketball, which was to have fun.

I did.

6

From the Nutty Receiver to a Flying Dutchman

When you're five-foot-nine or five-foot-ten, college basketball programs don't exactly come pounding on your door.

Despite my father's best efforts, my door stayed silent through my last two years at Garfield.

My father had spent hundreds of dollars getting me rated by some of the many national high school basketball scouting services out there. Colleges get your profile from a service and if they like what they see, they might take a second look.

There was interest from the University of New Haven, a Division 2 school, but no scholarship offer. Other schools also gave me feelers, but no scholarships.

I honestly wasn't hung up about the idea of getting a full ride—or even part of one—from anybody. Obviously, it was a big deal to my parents because they were the ones who would have to pay a lot of money to put two kids through college. Jen had already started at Glassboro State College (now called Rowan University) in southern New Jersey. She would later transfer to Rutgers University, from which she would graduate with honors.

I just wanted to keep playing sports while getting an education. I also figured, scholarship or not, being involved with athletics would help make up for whatever I might have lacked academically. I didn't have the best grades, but I had good grades.

I wasn't looking to make a career out of playing basketball. I didn't have these grand intentions of being Muggsy Bogues or Bobby Hurley. Basketball was just something I loved to play and I wanted to play as long as possible.

I was looking to go somewhere I knew I could make the team. And that meant checking out mostly small schools, which don't even have scholarships to offer.

What I kept finding, though, was that small schools and big schools saw the same thing when they looked at me—someone who wasn't tall enough to help their basketball programs.

So I began to have a change of heart. I still loved basketball, but the thought of not being able to play it on the collegiate level was discouraging. I told my father that it was time to refocus—time to take a look at what might be available for me in football. Again, I knew I wouldn't be seeing any scholarships, but I was hoping there might be an opportunity for me somewhere—anywhere.

When a couple of schools asked for a highlight videotape and we didn't have one, Dad immediately got cracking. We weren't a big school that had an audio and visual club taping our games, so this would have to be a homemade job.

Working from the tapes he had shot from the stands with his camcorder, my father put together all of my biggest plays from my three-year high school career. It wasn't exactly an NFL Films production. About half the shots were focused on the grass, the other half on the sky. Somewhere in there, you might see a few plays—some catches, some blocks, and my only kickoff return for a touchdown.

But most of the time, the camera would be shaking all over the place and all you could hear was my parents' cheering and jumping up and down. It was hysterical.

Thank God we left out the "highlights"—or lowlights—from my sophomore year when I first started playing. When I watched those tapes a couple of years later, I was thinking, *That can't be me out there, lining up in the wrong spot, running around like a chicken with its head cut off.* It looked like Jerry Lewis playing the part of the Nutty Receiver.

It was horrible.

. . .

After the frosty motorcycle ride my dad and I made to Muh-lenberg College, the next time I would see a college football game in person was just before my senior year of high school in September 1990.

My sister was dating a guy named Curt Geisler, who played defensive tackle at Fordham, so Dad and I went to see him play a Saturday night game at Hofstra in Hempstead, New York. I never even knew Hofstra, a Division 3 school at the time, existed before then.

The stadium was packed with more than five thousand people. Hofstra won, 35–16.

I thought, *I like this.* I liked the whole atmosphere— the crowd, the energy . . . it just felt right. I didn't give much thought to going to school there, but what I saw did give me something to think about, if only for comparison's sake.

Fordham, a Division 1-AA school, had shown a lot of interest in me. That seemed like it would be a great situation because Jen's boyfriend, Curt, was a good friend of mine. And I was even more convinced I should go there after visit-ing Curt on the campus in the Bronx.

I heard gunshots, I heard sirens . . . it was like being in the middle of any one of the fifteen *Lethal Weapon* movies. It was a happening place. I thought, *This is the life. This is where I should be.*

Then I found out that the tuition was twenty-two thousand dollars a year. I knew there was no way my parents were going to swing that when they were already paying four or five thousand a year to send my sister to a state school. I also knew, being a small school, there was not going to be a scholarship offer.

Another problem with Fordham was that the coaches weren't sure whether to play me on offense or defense. I wanted to play offense.

East Stroudsburg, a Division 2 school, and Bucknell and Lafayette—both Division 1-AA—were also interested in me. Coaches from all three places assured me that I would be able to play football as a freshman, but I didn't like the fact that they were way out in the sticks. I know I didn't grow up in action central. I just didn't like the thought of being that far out in the middle of nowhere.

One of Dad's tapes ended up at Hofstra. I guess the head coach, Joe Gardi, liked what he saw because he was pretty quick to call and see if I wanted to play for the Flying Dutchmen.

I never really made an official visit to Hofstra, but there was a lot I already liked about the place. Seeing what the Flying Dutchmen had done to Fordham's Rams at the game I had watched with my dad was a definite selling point. So was the fact they ran a run-and-shoot offense with four receivers on the field most of the time; I figured they would have to carry at least eight receivers on the squad.

I was also impressed that they were making the jump to Division 1-AA. They were still five years away from offering scholarships for football, which wasn't going to do me any good, but at least they were moving in the right direction.

The tuition wasn't quite as expensive as Fordham's, but at eighteen thousand dollars it also wasn't cheap.

I never lost sight of the fact that my main reason for enrolling at Hofstra was to get an education. A degree from Hofstra carries some pretty good weight in the working world. I don't know how sure my parents were that I would graduate, but they knew, if I did, I would have a great headstart when I set off on my own.

For me, there was one very good reason for leaving Hofstra with a diploma: I knew how much it was costing my parents. I knew they were spending more than triple the amount for my education than they were for Jen's. I wanted to do it right. I definitely wanted to get out of there on time, with a degree, so they wouldn't have to spend a dime more to put me through school.

My major was criminology/sociology. I've just always liked mysteries, trying to figure out all of the whodunits and why. I took some classes in crime and deviants. I studied serial killers, masterminds, the thinking of the police, the DEA, the CIA, and the FBI.

I thought, *Maybe I'll get a law enforcement job in the field*. I could never see myself working behind a desk. After eighteen years of living dangerously, I figured I might as well try to make a career of it.

As for football, my goals were fairly modest at first. The way my father and I saw it was, hopefully I could get some

playing time as a freshman, make the travel squad by my sophomore year, play a lot as a junior, maybe start as a senior.

The first game of my freshman year was a pretty unforgettable
experience. We were at home against Bucknell. It was a Friday
night, and just the idea of playing under the lights was excit-
ing.

It wasn't like being in Columbus, Ohio, to watch Ohio
State or in Knoxville, Tennessee, to watch the University of
Tennessee. There were probably five thousand people in the
stands, but the crowd was a hell of a lot larger than I had ever
seen at any game in high school. And they were on hand to
witness what would turn out to be a 36-point win.

I was way down on the depth chart and, as expected, all I
had done was watch from the sidelines. It wasn't until the
fourth quarter that the coaches put me in. As I said, I didn't go
to Hofstra expecting to be a starter or even a backup who
played regularly right off the bat. But after playing every play
on offense, defense, and special teams at Garfield, it felt a little
weird to suddenly be a garbage-time player.

On the first play I went in, there was no one covering me.
We had it set up in our offense where, if you were the hot receiver, the quarterback—who at the time was George Beisel—
would get a quick snap and just throw you the ball. That's how
it is in the run-and-shoot. It's run-and-gun all over the place.
Before I even had time to think about it, I had the ball in my
hands and I was just running down the field.

I wound up catching four passes in about ten plays. I thought, *I can do this.* Of course, that was before I sprained my collarbone and ended up making a trip to the hospital after the game to confirm it wasn't broken.

Beisel ended up going to the hospital with me because of a cut he suffered in the game that needed stitches. We sat in the emergency room as I tried to convince my father that I was fine and would be ready to play the following week.

It was common for us to use four and five receivers at a time. We had no tight ends on the team. We had no fullbacks or running backs. Besides the quarterback, the only other player in the backfield was what we called a superback, who was a combination fullback and running back and who had to be able to catch the ball. My roommate, Jeff Becchetti, played that position. He was the one who came out when we would go to five wides.

Coach Gardi and his staff had us run some crazy stuff in our run-and-shoot attack. On some plays, we would stack three receivers behind each other. Near the goal line, we would put all of our mooses in. The superback in those situations was one of our defensive tackles, a huge guy named Vinny Pisano, who was five-foot-ten and weighed at least 350 pounds. We called him "the Pizza Man." When he lined up next to our other tackle, Mike Gifford, also known as "Heavy G," there were six hundred and fifty pounds of beef in the middle of our defensive line. These guys not only would clog up the hole, but they could also move.

Playing receiver in the run-and-shoot is almost all catching. There is some blocking, but it mostly involves running routes and adjusting on the fly. If you're running down the field and you want to break in or curl into the left, you have to throw up your right arm. If you're breaking right, you throw up your left arm.

In that first year, I still didn't have a complete grasp of the game. I still didn't have a clue about what everyone was talking about when it came to the X's and O's, and I still was too proud—and too embarrassed—to ask. I just nodded like a fool. I was doing most everything right; I just didn't know why I was doing it.

So I decided at that point, if I was going to have any kind of success, I was going to have to figure out, once and for all, what football strategy and terminology were all about. I was going to have to become a student of the game. I wanted to learn all of the ins and outs of it. Instead of just memorizing the diagrams that I saw on the chalkboard and what to do once I was on the field, I was determined to understand.

Why, if you have the choice between running a flag route or a post against a Cover Three—where the secondary divides the field into thirds with the cornerbacks playing deep outside and the safety playing the deep middle—do you run the flag? Because you want to go to the hole between one of the corners and the safety. Why, if you have the choice between running a post pattern or a flag against a Cover Two—which is where you have two safeties deep and the corners underneath—do you run the post? Because the hole would be in the middle of the field, as opposed to Cover Three, when the safety is there.

The answers started coming in my sophomore year. It helped having suitemates like Brian Clark, who played safety, and Pat Shanahan, who played cornerback. I'd listen to them talk to each other all the time about the coverages they played in different situations and the reasons they played them. And by getting a handle on their responsibilities, I had a better idea of what would be to my advantage offensively. I learned a lot about offense by learning about defense.

I found it so much easier to ask those guys questions, away from the rest of the team, rather than the coaches. Brian—who is my closest friend and is trying to catch on with the San Diego Chargers after a successful career in the CFL—has been playing organized tackle football since he was in grammar school. His tremendous understanding of the game has rubbed off on me along the way.

Because of the type of offense we ran, all of the receivers had to know what everyone around them was doing in order not to end up in the same spot at the same time. We usually lined up with a guy on each side of the field. While one ran his route based on his read of the defense, the other ran more of a set pattern. The inside guys would also run their routes based on reads. I was all over the place—inside and outside, left and right—which gave me a chance to learn every spot. That helped me a lot once I got to the Jets, because knowing every receiver spot gave me more of a chance to make the team and be successful.

One downside of our pass-happy approach at Hofstra was that opponents knew we were throwing most of the time, so defenders could just tee off on us without worrying too much about stopping the run. They would give up the short patterns all day, then take their whacks to try and make us cough up the ball.

For me, hanging on was a challenge, especially early on. At five-foot-ten, I was as tall as I was going to get, but I was skinny, about 170 pounds. My body hadn't really matured yet. I had just started lifting. I was pretty much a stick out there, and it seemed that every defensive player I faced was determined to snap me in half.

I took their best shots. I collected a lot of bruises and welts, a few concussions, and other wounds that only hurt when I laughed—or tried to sit down.

But I usually hung on to the ball.

And, as always, I kept coming back for more.

7

"P.T."

Inspiration comes from many different sources and takes many different forms.

For me, the source is my maternal grandmother. The form is the lasting memory of her battle with cancer, which she lost at the end of my sophomore season at Hofstra.

Her name was Pauline Toth and I was closer to her than I was to any of my grandparents I knew. I never really had much contact with my father's parents. My mother's father died when she was ten, leaving my grandmother to raise her with the help of two older sons, my Uncle Gabe and my late Uncle Al.

For my sister and me, Grandma was like a second mother. She lived by herself in an apartment in Hasbrouck Heights and worked at Lodi Modern Bakery in Lodi, New Jersey. She was a strong, proud woman who never wanted to stop working and never wanted anyone's help to make ends meet.

Every Friday afternoon, as soon as we got out of school, my mother would drive us over to Lodi to pick up Grandma, along with a bag loaded with fresh buns and rolls. It was a ritual.

We always looked forward to her babysitting us whenever our parents went out because we basically were allowed to get away with murder. She almost always let us ignore the alleged bedtime my parents had set for us so we could watch TV. Grandma was so cool, she would actually stand in front of the window and as soon as she saw the headlights of their car, she would yell, "Here they come! Quick! Get into bed or you're going to get me in trouble!"

Not wanting to ruin a good thing, we would always jump into our beds and pretend to have been asleep for hours when our parents walked in the door. Then would hear my grandmother say, "No, they were angels. They went to bed a long time ago."

It was all we could do not to burst out laughing.

We thought we had them fooled. Little did we know that they were on to us—and her—all along. They just let us continue playing our little game because they knew it was a big part of the fun the three of us had together.

On the rare nights that we did go to bed before Dad and Mom got home, one of us would yell, "Grandma, we're hungry." And, using those great small rolls she would bring home from the bakery, she made each of us a sandwich of bologna, cheese, and mustard, then she delivered them to our beds. Of course, the whole time we were eating them she would say, in the sternest voice she had (which still wasn't the least bit threatening), "Don't you dare tell your mother I did this or she'll kill me."

You'd think that that would be good enough, but then, after finishing our sandwiches, we would ask her to rub or scratch our backs—fifty times each. No problem. Our wish was Grandma's command.

My sister and I weren't the only ones who made a mess of the house when my parents weren't home. I remember one time when Grandma fell asleep on the couch and left a glass pot of water she was boiling for tea burning on the stove. The pot, which didn't whistle, boiled for so long, the water evaporated and the pot caught on fire. Jen and I were too engrossed with whichever one of our favorite TV shows was on—"The Dukes of Hazard" or "Love Boat" or "Fantasy Island"—to pay any attention. That is, until my sister happened to see a reflection on the wall of the flickering flames.

We started screaming and yelling, "Grandma, Grandma, wake up! There's a fire in the kitchen!"

Grandma jumped off the couch, all in a panic. And the first thing she did was empty an entire tub of Morton's salt on the flames, which, of course, was the last thing she should have done because it only made them worse. Then she reached for my mother's good dishtowels, which also started to burn.

Eventually, she got the fire out. And after cleaning up the mess as best she could, Grandma warned us, "Don't you tell your parents about this or I will never be able to babysit you again."

Something tells me my mother was able to figure out what happened when she found her black pot in the garbage and black dishtowels in the sink.

Jen and I normally slept in separate rooms, but when my grandmother watched us, my sister usually slept on the bottom of my bunk beds, giving me ample opportunity to harass her. I would lean over and do all of the things that any little brat of a brother would do to his sister—spit, pick my nose, and throw boogers on her. I would also start jumping on my bed, causing the wooden slats to sometimes slip out of place and bringing the whole box spring and mattress crashing on top of her.

After Dad put in additional slats to keep that from happening, I had to find other means of harassment. So I removed the bar on the side of the bed that was supposed to keep me from falling out, leaned over, and resumed my disgusting assault. At one point, I leaned too far and the next thing my sister saw was my body flying past her, in what had to have been a good six-foot drop, and landing facefirst on the floor. She enjoyed having the last laugh—until she saw the blood pouring out of my nose.

Then it was Grandma to the rescue.

This sort of thing seemed to happen every time my grandmother babysat us. But by the time my parents got home, the bleeding would be stopped, everything would be cleaned up, and the three of us would maintain our code of silence. My parents would come home not knowing that a single thing had happened—or so we thought.

We were on equal footing with Grandma. We had as much dirt on her as she had on us.

Being the All-Pro hellion I was as a kid, I had my moments when I tried even Grandma's patience. On weekends, my sister and I would go to the mall with my mother and grandmother. We'd be someplace boring, like a clothing store, and it wouldn't be long before I did something wrong—touch something, hit my sister, whatever. Grandma would come after me, but I was too quick and elusive for her. I'd dive underneath one of those circular clothes racks. If she managed to flush me out of one, I'd dive under another. Then another. She could never catch me.

But she never could stay mad at me or anyone else.

This is the type of person Grandma was: If we wanted something, any kind of toy regardless of how silly it might have been, she would buy it for us. It didn't matter if she was down to her last ten bucks. It didn't matter if she needed to replenish her refrigerator or her cupboard.

"It's all right," Grandma would say to my mother's protests. "I don't need anything. Don't worry about it."

She was the sweetest, kindest, most generous person I

have ever known in my life. No one had any hard feelings toward her. I can't remember ever having the urge to get into an argument with her. In her eyes, my sister and I could do no wrong. We were angels and if my mother tried to tell her otherwise, she refused to listen.

"Not my eensies," she would say.

Grandma supported my sister and me in everything we did. When she was still able to get around, you could always count on her to be in the stands at one of our games, cheering us on with all of her heart.

It was sometime in 1990, during my senior year of high school, that Grandma was diagnosed with cancer. I remember taking off from school to go to the hospital with her and my mother when the doctor dropped that bombshell.

Maybe a lot of other teenagers, especially guys, couldn't be bothered or would just prefer not to be present for something like that, but staying away wasn't even an option. I didn't just feel I had to be there; I wanted to be there to give all of the support I could and just be a shoulder to cry on. It was the least I could do for someone who had always been there for everyone else—someone who had always done her best to try to hold together Mom and her brothers and all of our families through the roughest of times.

During my senior season, she actually came to some of my football games hooked up to a portable IV. But it was so tough for her to get around, and a couple of times, she fell. Between the cancer and her diabetes, it was that much more dangerous for her to take a fall because if she suffered any sort of cut or scrape, her body wouldn't heal. It got to the point where if she peeled off a Band-Aid, flesh would actually come off with it, leaving a half-inch gash that looked like a shark bite.

In the summer of 1992, just before the start of my sophomore season, Grandma took a turn for the worse. She was seventy-nine, and doctors were now measuring her life in weeks.

At the end of August, right after I finished preseason workouts, I made a trip home to see how she was doing. I wound up returning to school after bed check the night before our season opener against Central Connecticut State, and Coach Gardi gave me a one-game suspension. I thought I had a legitimate excuse, but he didn't want to hear about it. He took the rules-are-rules approach and, like it or not, I had to suffer the consequences. Because I was recovering from arthroscopic knee surgery that summer, I would have missed the game anyway.

But if I had been suspended for all of the games that year, it would have been worth it for the chance to see my grandmother.

By then, Grandma was pretty much confined to a wheelchair and the hospital-style bed set up for her at my Uncle Al's house in Rutherford. She needed to be lifted from bed to wheelchair, from wheelchair to bathroom, and whenever I was around, I'd do that for her. It felt odd at first, because I was so used to her carrying the load for me and carrying me around when I was little. All of a sudden, I was looking at this woman whom I had always considered the strongest woman in the world, and I was carrying her. At that point, I realized my grandmother was fighting a battle she wasn't going to win, yet I admired her greatly just for the fact she was still fighting.

And being the proud lady that she was, she couldn't hide the embarrassment she felt over her grandson seeing her in a state of almost total dependence—seeing her so weak and so frail as cancer continued to eat her life away.

"Grandma, don't worry, it's no big deal," I'd say. "You look beautiful."

Still, to see someone you admire and love so much go through something like that was very hard for everyone in our family. We are such a small tightly bound group and we feel each other's pain, as well as each other's joy.

Once the season began, I made regular trips home to visit Grandma. We usually played on Friday night, and I would head back to New Jersey on Saturday, which we had off.

Most of my grandmother's hair had been taken away by more than a year of chemotherapy. By midseason, whatever was left was also disappearing. When she spoke, it was pretty much gibberish. So I would just talk to her as I always did. I didn't know if she understood a word I was saying, and I really didn't care. I was just going to continue to keep her informed of everything I was doing, hoping that maybe one tiny piece of it would register and make her still feel connected in some way.

On November 7, 1992, we played our homecoming game against Dayton. We lost, but I ended up with two touchdown catches. I kept the ball after the second one and, using a black marker, I wrote on it: TO GRANDMA—TWO TOUCHDOWNS—I LOVE YOU. 11/7/92.

When I went to visit her the next day, she was more out of it than I had seen her the previous times. But I still tried to make a connection.

"Hey, Grandma, how are you doing?" I said. "It's Wayne John."

She and my mother liked to call me by my first and middle names so my father and I would know which of us was being summoned. When I was younger, I got summoned a lot—and usually not just to come home from whatever sport I was playing because dinner was on the table.

"I scored two touchdowns this week, and I have this ball for you," I said.

I read the inscription out loud, then placed the ball next to her on the bed. I swear, for a second, she seemed to actually smile, as if to tell me that she understood what was happening.

Even if she didn't, I'll always believe that she did.

Our final game of the season was at Montana. We lost, 50–6, but that didn't bother me nearly as much as the fact that I wouldn't be able to get home that weekend. We had played a Saturday game and had to stay over until Sunday because, with the distance involved, it was the earliest the school could book our return flight. We traveled all day Sunday, then I had classes the rest of the week.

At eleven o'clock Wednesday morning, my telephone rang. It was my father.

"Today is the day, Butch," he said.

He didn't have to say anything else. I knew exactly what he was talking about. November 18, 1992, was the day my grandma was going to die. To this day, I still don't understand how you would know something like that, but my parents and my uncles knew.

"I'm coming right now," I said.

"Take your time," Dad said. "Don't go crazy trying to get here."

"Listen, I'll be right over."

When I got there, I found my sister crying and my mom and everyone else there very upset. Grandma was still alive, but just barely. The scene was so ironic because everybody was kind of falling apart, and the one person who had always held things together in the Toth family couldn't do anything about it.

I walked up to Grandma's bed. Her eyes were closed and she was breathing in quick, heavy gasps.

Six hours later, at around seven o'clock that night, my mom and her two brothers walked into my grandmother's bedroom and stood along the side of the bed. I followed them in, then shut the door behind me.

For as long as I live, I will never forget what I witnessed. Grandma was lying on her side, looking beautiful. Her hair was gone. Her face was covered with sweat.

There was an eerie silence. The only sound was Grandma's breathing, which was much slower and halting than before. We waited for her to take one more gasp . . . then another . . . then another.

Then, all of a sudden, she just stopped.

It was the weirdest feeling ever, watching someone die like that right before your eyes.

My first reaction was a sense of relief that her suffering was over and that she had gone to a better place. I never actually cried that day. I was only nineteen, but I felt emotionally strong. I drew from the strength that my grandmother, the strongest woman I have ever known, instilled in me. Right then, I knew I was supposed to take all of that strength and use it to look after her three kids—just try to be a sturdy rock that they could lean on at a time when they needed it the most.

Grandma's dying did a lot to bring my mother and me closer together—as close as my father and I had always been. There was a time when I had so many arguments with my mom—usually because I would do or say something stupid to really anger her—that Grandma felt more like a mother to me than she did.

But after we got home from the funeral, my mom wrapped her arms around me and started crying. And at that moment, as we held each other, I vowed that I would never do anything to hurt my mom again.

Whenever I'm by myself and truly alone with my thoughts, I frequently think about my grandmother's fight with cancer. I think about the inner strength and dignity she showed right until the very end.

If I'm ever having a bad day on the field, I'll say to myself,

Listen, if Grandma could fight off death for as long as she did and make it through a whole football season, what is ever going to be so bad in my life that I can't overcome?

That's why before each game I've played since my junior year at Hofstra, I've taken a marker and written P.T., my grandmother's initials, on the top of my left shoe and drawn an arrow pointing forward—but actually meant to be pointing upward, toward heaven—on the other.

Anytime you feel tired in a game, the natural instinct is to put your hands on your knees and look to the ground. When I do that and see those initials and that arrow, I think, *I'm tired? What is that? I'm alive, I'm playing football, my family is watching. I think I'm tired?*

Forget it!

When anyone happens to notice the P.T. on my shoes, the first question I hear is: "What is that for? Prime Time?"

"No," I say. "It's my grandma's initials."

I usually get a puzzled look until I explain how much she had meant to me and how inspiring it is for me just to see those initials during the course of a game.

But my shoe isn't the only place P.T. appears. I also have it permanently engraved on the inside of my left forearm. I did it myself, using a disposable razor, then a screwdriver to make sure it would scar well enough to be visible. I know that sounds a little crazy, but I had what I believe was a good reason for doing it. In April of 1997, *Sports Illustrated* was putting together an article about me and had arranged to take some photographs of me doing everyday things around the house in the offseason. The piece was supposed to deal quite a bit with the important role my grandmother still played in my life and my football career. Then suddenly there was a change of plans. Because *SI* wanted it to be more of a happy, upbeat piece, Grandma was completely eliminated from the article. I understood it. I wasn't happy about it, but I understood it.

So, to be certain she would still appear in the magazine, I decided to give myself a little tattoo, then I made sure my left forearm was visible in every photograph taken for the layout. Did it hurt? Let's put it this way, if you believe in why you're doing something, then it isn't painful.

In March of 1999, I got a professional tattoo of PAULINE in my grandma's handwriting. Above it is the Chinese symbol for family; below it is the date of her death, 11-18-92. The handwriting sample was from one of the letters she used to write every day to Jen the first year my sister was away at college. Each one contained an update on what happened on the soap opera "General Hospital," which Jen missed while she was in class.

A lot of players have initials or other personal messages in the form of a tattoo or written with a marker on their shoes or maybe on the tape around their wrists or ankles—anything that they can look at during a game for a little bit of inspiration. It is just something that helps give you strength from within—strength that you don't believe you have until you focus your thoughts the right way.

You wouldn't believe how far stuff like that can carry you.

I realize some guys don't feel they need to rely on anything of the sort. I realize some are just so physically blessed that they don't ever have to bear down because they believe they will always be carried by their skills. Maybe so.

But there are other people, like myself, that have always had to work so much harder for what we achieve. We're the ones who constantly seek something, no matter how insignificant it might seem to someone else, to give us an edge over an opponent.

There is such a fine line between failing and succeeding, between winning and losing, and the difference isn't always determined by how much size, speed or strength you're blessed with.

I've had people say to me sometimes, "Look at you, you're only five-foot-ten."

I'll say, "Well, that has nothing to do with it. You can't measure my heart and you can't measure my brain. Those are what will carry me through. My height has nothing to do with it."

That goes for anyone, not just athletes. If someone wants a pay raise but shows the boss even the slightest doubt in his or her abilities, then he or she isn't going to get it.

That is a fact of life.

By keeping Grandma's memory with me at all times, I will never be too tired or too weak on the field. There is nothing I won't be able to do because I know she is behind me all the way.

I know she is always watching down on me.

8

The Need for Speed

In the ladder of organized sports, the higher you climb, the more you have to deal with labels.

In football, size is huge—especially when the player isn't. If you're tagged "too small," it sticks with you forever.

Speed is another favorite category. If you're stamped "too slow," you might as well be carrying a turtle shell on your back.

Each year at Hofstra, the first day of preseason workouts

was devoted to speed testing, in which the coaches timed us in the forty-yard dash. We did it track style, right out of the blocks. Having never run track, my times obviously weren't going to stack up very well against some of the other receivers who had track backgrounds—guys like Michael Wright and Aric McEachin. Aric was a sprint champion in the Empire State Games. I was practically starting from a standstill because I didn't know how to get into a proper three-point sprinter's stance.

So while Aric was running his forties in 4.3–4.4, I was running mine in 4.7–4.8.

I was fast when I needed to be fast—on the field. But that didn't seem to mean all that much to our offensive coordinator, Manny Matsakis. He took one look at the way I ran in the preseason, then made up his mind that I didn't have the kind of speed he was looking for. I didn't resent the fact that there were other guys on the team who did. It had nothing to do with the other guys. It was about the coordinator's perception of me based on what he saw on his stopwatch.

Matsakis came to Hofstra from a big-time program, Kansas State, where he coached receivers. He brought along a philosophy that if a receiver didn't have great speed, he might as well not have hands, legs, or anything else. He was determined to play his fastest guys as much as possible.

Even though I was always one of the fastest players on my high school team and had caught thirty-six passes in my first two college seasons, I was stuck in the fourth spot on the depth chart. I never once saw the starting lineup as a sophomore.

I was frustrated. I couldn't deal with being on the team and not being a central part of it. This had nothing to do with ego or wanting to be in the spotlight. It was about fairness. I had worked so hard and caught the ball well enough, I thought, to deserve more playing time.

But it just seemed like there was no way for me to get past Matsakis's obsession with track speed. Finally I said to myself, *I can't work with this guy.* While driving with my father on the way home from school at the end of my sophomore year, I told him that I was seriously thinking about quitting the team.

"I don't think you want to do that, Butch," he said.

"But I just can't win with this guy."

"You're going to encounter guys like this all the time. You just have to prove him wrong."

Eventually, Dad talked me into sticking it out, which, deep down in my heart, I was probably looking for him to do anyway.

How ironic is that? The man who didn't want me to play football in high school, who wasn't going to sign that permission form, now was the one convincing *me* to keep playing the game in college.

To say the least, we're both very happy he succeeded.

Beginning in June of 1993, about two months before our preseason camp, I rededicated myself to improving every aspect of my game—especially my speed.

I had it in my mind that I wanted to start as a junior. I

wanted to be on the field as much as possible. I wanted to perform better than anyone else who would be competing for a receiver spot.

But in order for that to happen, I knew I had to be ready—physically and mentally. When I reported to camp, I didn't want there to be a shred of doubt in anyone's mind that I should be starting.

I needed more power and explosiveness in my legs, so the first step was changing my weight-lifting program. I began to concentrate on my lower body, which was something I had never really done before. I had always used basketball, biking, and running for that. Now I added squats and power cleans to my daily weight-lifting regimen.

I also began a running program designed to help further build my leg muscles. I had watched films that showed Jerry Rice and Walter Payton running up and down hills during their training. I started to do the same around the hilly terrain that surrounds my parents' home in Wanaque.

Running uphill is great for adding power and explosion because it helps build the muscles in the front of your legs. Running downhill helps increase the length of your stride because, with the acceleration caused by the incline, you learn to stride out as far as you can—or fall on your face. The longer your stride, the more ground you tear up. Of course, that didn't do much good on those downhill runs if I caught my toe in a hole and went tumbling ass over teakettle, which happened more than a few times.

To make things even more challenging, I did most of my

workouts at night. I'm talking midnight, one o'clock in the morning. After a day of working one of my summer jobs—landscaping or house painting—I'd usually be home at night, watching something on television. And that was when I would get the urge to start working out.

I knew I just couldn't spend a whole night sitting in front of the TV set. If I found myself doing that, I'd think, *No one else is sitting around. I know the other guys going out for receiver are working out somewhere right this second. They're busting their butts, trying to make themselves the best players they can be. And they're going to be ready when the season starts. So what am I doing on this damn couch? I have to get out there. I have to work even harder.*

I would get myself so upset that I had to put on my workout stuff and do something. Occasionally, it would just be some sit-ups, but most of the time it was an intensive period of running or riding my bike around nearby Lakeland Regional High School. I'd be tearing through the fields in almost total darkness, except for the distant glow of the streetlights.

The other thing I liked about working out late at night is that you're all alone; everything's quiet and there are no interruptions. When it's just you out there pushing yourself, that is when you work the hardest.

A lot of times I would jog from one end of the football field to the other, then turn around and sprint the whole way back into the darkness. Sometimes I would make believe someone was chasing me. Or I might put myself in a game situation: *Fourth down. Final seconds ticking away. Get into the end zone, Wayne, or we lose.*

At first, my parents would say, "You shouldn't do this at night when you can barely see. It's dangerous. Do it during the day."

But after I explained to them my need to outwork the competition, they understood. So while they were inside, counting Z's, I was outside, cutting, juking, and spinning around imaginary defenders. I was also trying to sidestep the goose shit that was all over the field, at least what I could see of it in the dark.

I have always demanded a lot more from myself than anyone could ever demand from me. I have always pushed myself a lot harder than anyone could ever push me.

Aside from contact drills, what the coaches put us through—physically and mentally—during two weeks of two-a-day practices was nothing compared to what I had put myself through in the two months leading up to preseason workouts.

Between improving the strength in my legs and teaching myself how to run out of the blocks, I was ready for the forty-yard dash at the start of preseason workouts before my junior year. And I proved it by running a 4.49.

I still wasn't starting, although part of that was because of a little setback I had when I suffered a concussion in a scrimmage that forced me to miss our opener.

But through the first few weeks of the season, it was becoming clear that a change in the receiving corps was in order.

The coaches started noticing the benefits of my stepped-up training routine. Not only was I faster, but I was stronger and I had a lot more endurance. I was also feeling a lot more comfortable with how my physical skills matched up with those of my opponents.

The breakthrough game of my college career came when we played Lehigh in the third week of the season. We were getting stomped through the entire first half, so the coaches knew they had to shake things up. I wound up starting in the second half and went on to catch thirteen passes for two hundred and five yards and two touchdowns. The yards were the most by a Hofstra player since Bill Starr's school-record two hundred and nineteen against Temple in 1965. We still lost, 31–24, but the comeback showed everyone the potential we had to strike quickly and often.

From the fourth game on, I became a full-time starter. I finished the season with fifty-seven receptions for seven hundred and eighty-eight yards and a team-high nine touchdowns. It was nice to see that some of that hard work had paid off, but I was far from satisfied. I was prepared to put myself through another summer of hell to try to better my performance from the previous year.

After my junior season, Matsakis returned to Kansas State to coach special teams and was replaced as offensive coordinator by Mike McCarty, who came from Southeast Missouri State, where he had been the passing game coordinator. For me, it was a godsend because this man was one of the best coaches I have ever had in my life.

McCarty believed in spreading the ball around more evenly and throwing more deep passes. He had us throw deep at least once a quarter.

"I don't care if we complete it," he would say. "I just want to stretch the defense out."

I liked that tenacity.

And I loved his decision to play me exclusively outside as a senior. McCarty appreciated the fact that I wanted the ball in my hands as much as possible. By putting me outside, where I could usually get open deep, he created a natural combination between me and our quarterback that year, Carlos Garay, who had one of the strongest passing arms I have ever seen. He got the ball to you so fast, you didn't have a choice but to catch it. It kind of caught you. I remember when Aric McEachin tried to catch one of Carlos's passes in practice and ended up with a broken thumb. I mean, the thumb was bent so far backward, it was touching the wrist.

Soon after that, he was switched to defensive back.

Carlos and I worked well together. I told him, "If you're ever in trouble, just throw it. I promise you that I won't let anyone intercept it. I will tackle the guy—whatever it takes—but they are not going to catch the ball if I can't."

And that was exactly how it was. I came down with most of Carlos's passes. The few times I didn't, I would draw a pass interference penalty. Both outcomes were better than an INT.

Besides a great friendship, Carlos and I developed a great chemistry on the field. In my senior year, it was just magical when we were out there. Everybody knew he was going to throw the ball to me—especially the opposing defense—but we still connected. That was mainly because he had such an excellent arm that it didn't take a lot to get open. All you had to do was be open for a second and he would put the ball in your hands. When I was double-covered, I knew that if I could just run past the defenders—which I usually could in my last two years at Hofstra—Carlos would be able to make the long throw for a big play.

If he happened to have a bad throw, I could almost always adjust and make the tough catch to compensate for him. If I ran a bad route or didn't get far enough away from the defensive back, he could almost always make a great throw and compensate for me.

McCarty and Dante Wright, the receivers coach who came with Mike to Hofstra from Southeast Missouri State, did the most to turn the lights on for me, so to speak, in terms of my understanding of football. They did a great job of explaining not only what we did but why we were doing it. Even if something didn't work, they would want us to keep doing it because it set the defense up for something else.

Wright knew the ins and outs of the receiver position. He was a younger guy, in his mid- to late twenties, who had recently played football at Southeast Missouri State. The majority of coaches you run into at all levels have never played the game. That doesn't make them bad coaches, but there is a lot to be said for hearing instruction from a person who has played the game before—someone telling you how to do a certain thing and then giving you a step-by-step demonstration.

Wright's emphasis was on shifting your weight downward when you made your cuts so that you could come out of your break as quickly as you got into it. A lot of guys kind of stand up as they run an in cut or an out cut, which forces them to slow down when they come out of their break and makes it easier for the defensive back to close on the play. Also, by keeping your chest over your feet, Wright pointed out, you can better maintain your balance and be that much quicker out of your break.

Those teachings still apply today. I am constantly working on my routes, as well as on every other aspect of my game. My laboratory is the practice field. Practice is where you can experiment with things that you're not ready to try in a game. If you try ten things in practice and one works, you have the confidence to use it when it counts. A spin move. A stiff-arm. A head fake. If it works in practice, against guys that you face every day and who know all of your tendencies, it is almost sure to work in a game.

Since I've been with the Jets, Aaron Glenn, who is one of the top cornerbacks in the league, and I try to go against each other as much as we can in practice. After four years of running the same routes against him, he knows exactly what I'm going to do on a certain pattern and vice versa. So it makes me work that much harder to come up with new ways to get open and it makes Aaron work that much harder to find new ways to stop me.

Practice is the hard part. Playing is the easy part.

•   •   •

The last game of my senior season was at Delaware. Our record was 8–1. A victory would help our chances of being selected for the NCAA Division 1-AA playoffs.

I approached the game as if we were not going to make it,
even if we did win. It wasn't that I lacked faith in our team or
in myself. I wanted to believe otherwise. I just don't count on
anything that I can't control. And since none of us was part of
the selection committee, getting a playoff bid was out of our
hands.

So as far as I was concerned, this would be the last organized football game I would ever play.

I have always loved to compete. For three years in high
school, I competed in three sports on an organized basis.
Then, when I got to college, I went from three sports to one.
Now I was going from one to none.

I just couldn't believe that this was going to be it.

I hadn't given a single thought to trying to play pro football. At least not a serious one. I mean, it wasn't as if NFL
scouts or sports agents were flocking to Hofstra to check me
out. Besides, I have never been one to live for the future. I'd
rather live for the day.

My philosophy has always been to make the most of every day that I'm alive.

I was going to lay it all on the line that day, which is the
approach I take to every game. But this wasn't every game. It
was going to be my farewell party and I planned on getting the
best I could out of this bash.

And that was exactly what I did. I had a career day, catching fourteen passes for a school-record two hundred and forty-

five yards and five touchdowns, which tied the 1-AA record Jerry Rice set at Mississippi Valley State. Three of the TDs came in the first quarter. I could have actually had six for the game if I hadn't been interfered with on a slant-go route. The guy was all over me, finally tripping me up to draw the flag, but I still hung on to the ball for a forty-yard gain. If I could have stayed on my feet, I would have been gone for another six points.

We truly were Flying Dutchmen that day. On the second play of the game, I had a hitch-and-go that went for about sixty yards. Then I had a slant that I took into the end zone from about the twenty-five. It was just one of those days where I caught every ball that came my way, no matter where it was thrown. It didn't even feel like I was playing. I felt like I was watching myself out there. I could do no wrong. You always hear athletes talking about being in the zone.

I was in the zone that day.

We played Delaware to a 41–41 tie, which, as most of us suspected after the game, did not convince the selection committee to invite us to the playoffs. (About a week later, we got the official word when 8–2–1 Alcorn State, with the great Steve McNair at quarterback, was chosen to face top-seeded Youngstown State.)

For the second year in a row, I caught fifty-seven passes for a school-record twelve hundred yards, the fourth-highest total in Division 1-AA that season. In all, I set six Hofstra records, including sixteen touchdown catches. I ranked third in Division 1-AA with a hundred and twenty receiving yards per game. I ranked fifth in scoring with 9.8 points per game. I would go on to become the thirteenth recipient of Hofstra's Iron Mike Award, honoring me as the Most Valuable Player of the 1994 season.

For my career, I had one hundred and fifty receptions for two thousand, two hundred and ninety-seven yards—which both rank second on the school's all-time career list—and a Hofstra-record thirty-one touchdowns.

But none of those accomplishments mattered as the final gun sounded in that Delaware game. There were no playoffs in our future, but at least I was satisfied that I had given everything I had—physically and emotionally—to try to make that a reality.

Between stopping to talk to other players and exchanging hugs with my fellow seniors, I was the last one to leave the field that day. As I began to walk off—holding my helmet at my side and with the eyeblack smeared on my sweat-covered face—I took my mouthpiece and set it on the ground. I figured, *Since this is the last game I'm ever going to play, I'll just leave it here. I'm not going to need it anymore.*

So many thoughts were swirling through my head. It was as if my entire athletic career were flashing before my eyes. It was the culmination of everything I had ever done at every level of sports, going back to when I first played catch with my father.

It was the longest walk of my life.

The first member of my family I spotted waiting for me was Jen. As soon as I saw her, I just lost it. I busted out in tears, she busted out in tears, and we threw our arms around each other. It was probably the hardest I have ever cried in my life.

The thing you have to understand about my sister is that she is very emotional, especially around me. If I smile, she smiles. If one tear hits my eye, a million pour out of hers. We're not twins, yet we have that kind of bond. Even if we win and I don't have such a good game, she is upset for me. She can feel worse for me than I can ever feel for myself.

Jen and I must have hugged for ten minutes that day, and I don't think either of us said a word the whole time. We didn't have to.

We both knew it was an ending, and we just weren't ready to let it go.

It wasn't long after the Delaware game that my father posed the following question to me: "What do you want to do, Butch? Do you want to play in the pros?"

"Well, yeah," I said. "But I know that won't happen. No one's going to give a guy my size from a school this small a chance to play in the NFL."

That wasn't the answer he was looking for. He wanted a yes or a no. If I said yes, that meant he was going to work like crazy to try to get me that chance, just as he did when we were looking at colleges, and he and my mother would support me for three years or until I made a team. If I said no, I could pursue a job in law enforcement and work at the collection agency until I found one.

My answer was yes.

"Do what you've got to do," I told my father.

"That's all I need to hear," Dad said.

If nothing else, I saw it as one more opportunity—no matter how remote—to play organized sports. The empty feeling I had walking off the field for what I thought was the last time was still fresh in my mind. There was no way I could stop myself from at least trying to get a shot.

It also gave me something to fill my daydreams. I wasn't thinking about fame or wealth. I was just thinking about being on another team, about putting on a uniform and a helmet one more time. If you do that as an adult and you're not playing football in the pros or in college, people start to look at you kind of funny.

After the horrible response my dad got from sending all thirty NFL teams the homemade highlight videotape of my games he recorded from cable TV, my agent, Art Weiss, entered the picture.

I was impressed with Art from the day he FedEx'd a letter to my locker at Hofstra, introducing himself and asking if I would be interested in having him represent me. No other agent had sent me a letter like that through regular mail, let alone via overnight delivery. My father had written to a couple of them, but never got a reply.

Art had a bunch of things going for him right off the bat: One, he was a graduate of Hofstra Law School; two, he had been an agent for about four years and his client list included one of my all-time favorite Giant players, linebacker Gary Reasons; three, he had seen me play enough to have an idea whether there was any hope whatsoever of my playing in the NFL.

I later found out that Art had shown Gary a videotape of me in action, just to get another outside opinion besides his own. Working as a color commentator for ABC's college football coverage at the time, Gary had seen a lot of the receivers from big-time schools play in big-time games.

"How does this kid react when he is in bump-and-run coverage?" Gary asked Art.

"It's funny you should mention that, because that was the first question I had," Art said. "And from what I see, he is not just losing people with quickness or moves; he is very strong. He can take a chuck at the line and still get loose."

"If this guy can play bump-and-run, he is a hell of a prospect. Because this guy is as good as I've seen this year."

Too bad Gary wasn't a general manager or player personnel director in the NFL.

In December of 1994, about two weeks after I got Art's letter, Dad gave him a call and the two of us went to see him at his office in Franklin Lakes, which is only ten minutes from Wanaque. Up to that point, Stu Hermann, a CPA whose office is in the same building as my parents' collection agency, was working with my father to get someone from an NFL team to notice me. Stu is a great guy and he was trying to be helpful, but he was out of his element. If we were going to do this right, we realized we had to hook up with someone who knew his way around the game and what buttons to push.

Not that Art was offering any guarantees. In fact, from the very start, he was frank and up-front about my prospects.

"Listen, this is going to be a roll-up-your sleeves type of thing," Art told my father. "There are no promises here. We'll be swimming upstream the whole way. But I think he has the ability. I really believe in him. I'm prepared to be his advocate and do what it takes to get him looked at. But he has to do the rest."

That seemed like a pretty fair proposition to both of us. Art was hired.

For the next several weeks and months, he shipped out my tape to almost every professional football organization in existence. Whenever he would run out of tapes, all he had to do was call my father, who would come rushing over with ten more.

The plan was to get me a workout somewhere so that maybe I could get drafted in April of that year or signed as a free agent a day or two later.

I didn't really know it at the time, because Art didn't want to discourage me too much, but it seemed that whenever he put my name out there, someone would slam it right back in his face. When he mentioned it to two of the more important men in the football scouting business—Jack Butler of Blesto, which is based in Pittsburgh, and Duke Babb of National Football Scouting, which is based in Tulsa, Oklahoma—they basically said, "Wayne who?"

The first question asked by most pro scouts is: "Where did he go to school?"

"Hofstra."

"Ewww!"

"How tall is he?"

"Five-foot-ten."

"Ewww! That means he's really five-foot-four because we all know how much these schools like to exaggerate."

"How much does he weigh?"

"A hundred and eighty."

"Ewww! That means he's really a hundred and seventy-five, soaking wet."

So right away, I have three strikes against me and they haven't even met me. Forget about my stats. Forget about my highlight video. All they want to know is: Where did you go to school, how tall are you, and how much do you weigh?

They rate players on a piece of paper. They don't know if you're black, white, orange, or green. They don't know the person or what's inside of him. But that is just the way the scouting business is, which I understand. So many people get overlooked because it's a big country and it's impossible to go to every school, check out every player, look under every stone.

When "Hofstra" and "five-foot-ten" pop up, with no other background or feel for me as a player, a name like mine automatically turns to mud. General managers would say things to Art like, "Hey, pal, if you want to stay in this business and have any credibility, you had better not get on the side of a guy like this."

"But you know what?" Art would say years later. "If you are a lawyer long enough, you're told things like that every day in every forum—a courtroom or whatever. That never discouraged me. If anything, it lit a fire under me. I'm the kind of guy that if you say no, it pisses me off so much that I really want to go after it."

Who does that sound like?

Art would always tell me, "Keep in shape. Keep your head up. I believe something is going to happen here. It is going to break for you."

You had to love the guy. There he was, taking crap from all corners on my behalf—with no assurance that he would even see dime one for his trouble—and he still hung in there with me. My family and I have never forgotten that.

I wasn't invited to play in any college all-star games. I certainly wasn't going to get an invitation to the NFL's annual scouting combine in Indianapolis.

That left workouts, such as those I had to pay to attend in Baltimore and at Rutgers, to try to get someone's attention. But each one was like every player who showed up for them—a real long shot.

The only time I felt even the tiniest bit of promise was when I worked out for Jim Garrett, a New Jersey-based scout for the Dallas Cowboys, in Red Bank. He not only told me he thought I had a chance to make an NFL team—maybe not the Cowboys, but a team—he also gave me a strong recommendation to his son John, a receivers coach for the Cincinnati Bengals. The Bengals were planning to use a low-round draft pick or two on a receiver that year.

That conversation with Jim made me a whole lot more

enthusiastic about this whole process of saying, "Hey, look at me! Look at me! I can play for you!"

Art did everything he could to try to create a market for me that wasn't there. He tried to scare up as many letters of recommendation as possible. One of the better ones came from former Jets defensive lineman Marty Lyons, who saw my games at Hofstra as a color analyst for SportsChannel.

"I truly believe that Wayne Chrebet, number 3 of Hofstra University, is a young man that . . . can play in the NFL and also be a pleasant surprise to any organization he plays for," Marty wrote. "It is my professional opinion that [he] has the tools, the heart, the character, and the leadership that the NFL looks for from all of its players."

Sometimes Art would stretch the truth a little. No, he didn't go around telling people I was six-foot-two and could run the forty in 4.3. At some point, a scout is going to be able to figure out that those numbers are a bit exaggerated—unless he's blind.

But what Art would do was take every letter we received from an NFL team, no matter how general it was, and include it in every package he shipped out to other clubs. And he would make the point in his cover letter and follow-up phone call that "Hey, look, there is another team checking this guy out," when, in reality, most teams were just answering with form letters out of courtesy.

One time Art did a little creative editing on a form letter from the Giants that didn't have my name or address on it. It just said "Dear Prospect" and gave information about their annual Stadium Day, which wasn't even a real workout but just a weigh-in and a chance to view their highlight film. Whoever typed the original had left a big space between the date and "Dear Prospect," so Art typed in my name and address there to give the impression the Giants had sent a personal letter to me. Then he ran off copies of it and stuck one into each package. He figured it might make a good impression on personnel people at other teams.

In fact, one college scouting director said to Art, "This guy must be special because they addressed it right to him."

"Yep," Art said, trying to keep a straight face. "He is that kind of a kid."

Art was just doing what it took to generate some interest in me, and sometimes that took a little creativity. He just did what he had to do to make sure that letter got into the right hands.

As Art always told me, "If you can't get a guy to the table, he can't eat."

In Art's letters to coaches and personnel types in the NFL, he would write things like "Wayne has attracted considerable attention from a number of NFL teams" and "In addition to the Giants, Jets, and Eagles—who are aware of Wayne in this area—I have been contacted by four NFL teams who have requested additional tape on Wayne."

Art would be the first to admit that those were very generous interpretations of the level of enthusiasm for me. At that point, I'd have been happy if just one team allowed me to come to its training camp—as a participant, not a spectator.

9

When a Draft Feels Like a Cold Shoulder

There are about one hundred and fifty players in the National Football League who will never forget the weekend of April 22–23, 1995.

They can tell you where they were and what they were doing the exact moment, during those forty-eight hours, that they got The Call—the one from the NFL team that had just drafted them.

I can tell you where I was and what I was doing that weekend, too.

On April 22, I was down at the Jersey Shore with my parents and my sister. My sister and I were hanging out, and while she was shopping I stopped into a little bar to grab a bite to eat.

ESPN's live coverage of the draft was on television. So, as I sat there, devouring my meatball sandwich, I took in all the fast-paced action of NFL commissioner Paul Tagliabue walking from the podium to grab a little slip of paper, then walking back to the podium to tell the rest of the world which first-round draft pick was going where.

I had always been a pretty big football fan, and I actually loved watching the draft. I kept up with who the top college prospects were and the needs each team had. I could tell you all about the "blue-chippers" and the "sleepers," the guys whose stock was rising and the guys who were fading fast.

Of course, my reason for watching that particular draft was a lot different than it had been in any other year. At that point, the last guy from Hofstra to even get a whiff of the NFL was a linebacker named Erik Ringoen, a tenth-round draft pick of the Seattle Seahawks in 1991. He was cut at the end of his first training camp.

When you play at Hofstra, no one ever calls you a "blue-chipper." You've never even been considered awake long enough to be a "sleeper." You don't rise, so there's nowhere to fall.

Obviously, I wasn't waiting for The Call on the first day. I can't say that I was really expecting it on the second day, ei-

ther, but the Bengals, through the Garrett father-son connection, had given us at least a tiny bit of hope that they might
make me a low-round choice. In fact, after they traded with
Carolina for the top overall pick and used it to take Penn State
running back Ki-Jana Carter, I said to myself, *Maybe I'm going to
be teammates with that guy.*

Later in the first round, the Jets chose another Nittany
Lion, Kyle Brady. Everybody started to boo. You heard it from
the crowd at the draft in New York, as well as from the people
in the bar. For one thing, the Jets still had Johnny Mitchell, another tight end who had been their number-one pick a few
years earlier. For another, Warren Sapp, a big defensive lineman from the University of Miami who would eventually end
up going to Tampa Bay and making the Pro Bowl, was still
available.

I had never been that big a Jet fan to react one way or the
other. I just looked at Brady on that TV screen, and for a brief
moment, it didn't feel so bad to be watching someone else get
drafted—even on the first round.

I thought to myself, *This poor guy. He doesn't know what he's
getting into.*

I watched the second day of the draft from the family room of
my parents' home. This time I didn't feel like another fan anymore. I was hoping that maybe the Bengals, New Orleans, or
some other team that might go for a receiver in the late rounds
would give me the chance I was hoping for.

This time I was waiting for The Call.

We had told everyone we knew—every friend and relative—not to call the house that day, just to make sure the line would be clear and that we would know—if the phone ever did ring—someone from an NFL team would probably be at the other end.

Unless, of course, we heard from one of those people trying to sell us insurance or give us a new credit card.

I just wanted a chance. I'm the kind of guy, if you give me a crack, I'm going to turn it into the Grand Canyon. Up to that point, there weren't many things that I had not been able to do on a football field. As far as I was concerned, everything I had done at Hofstra I could do as a pro.

I also wanted to make my family proud. My father and mother and sister had been with me through every phase of this. They wanted it for me every bit as much as I wanted it for myself . . . maybe more.

On every team I had been on to that point, I played for my teammates, who were like brothers to me, but I also played for my real family. I played to make them proud. I played to give them something to be happy about. I played for the Chrebet name, which incidentally, means "mountaintop" in Ukrainian.

That attitude might sound a little corny to some people, but it meant a great deal to me. It still does.

Dad, Mom, Jen, Art, Amy, and I called ourselves the Society of True Believers. We were a very tight circle of people who believed that I could make it in the NFL—and who were prepared to be laughed at a lot.

The fifth round came, and as expected, the Bengals took a

receiver. Unfortunately, they didn't take the one all of us in that family room were praying they would take. They selected David Dunn of Fresno State. I guess they liked him for his kick-returning ability, which wasn't really my specialty but was something I would have been willing to try if it got me any closer to an NFL camp. Whatever the reason, we all knew that I had just been passed over by the one and maybe only team that seemed to have the greatest interest in drafting me.

I was crushed.

I later found out that just before the Bengals' pick came up, John Garrett, their receivers coach, had called Art Weiss at his home to say how sincerely disappointed he was that they wouldn't be drafting me.

"It's out of my hands," Garrett said. "We didn't expect David Dunn to be available, so we are going to take him. It happened at another level. It's just one of those things."

On the sixth round, the Saints also picked up a receiver. His name was Lee De Ramus, from Wisconsin. The only thing I knew about this guy was that he hadn't even played as a senior because of a broken leg he suffered in a noncontact drill before the season. The Saints were hoping—*hoping!*—that after he finished his rehabilitation, he would be ready for training camp.

I'm sitting there saying, "Can you believe this? Now they're drafting guys with broken legs? At least I have two healthy legs here."

The seventh and final round came and went without the phone ringing once.

Thirty NFL teams had just handed out two hundred and

forty-nine invitations to college players, thirty-one of them wide receivers, to try to make their rosters. And none of them thought I was good enough to get one.

Even though my family and I thought it was a slim possibility that I would be picked, I still felt embarrassed. I felt like I was letting down the people I cared about the most. I knew they were feeling pretty awful, too. Not for themselves, but for me.

But I also knew that all wasn't completely lost.

When the draft ends, that's when teams start rounding up rookie free agents. It's called the draft after the draft. This time, we all thought, the phone was definitely going to ring.

Once again, though, it just sat there in dead silence. Every second felt like an hour. And all I could say to my family was: "I'm sorry, I'm sorry."

"You've got nothing to apologize for," Mom said. "They don't know what they're missing."

Spoken like a true mother.

Finally, around eight o'clock that night, about two hours after the draft, the phone rang. We all looked at each other, sort of half smiling with all sorts of feelings running through us. There was relief. There was hope. And there was a little bit of fear that maybe, just maybe, we were going to find out that no one wanted me, not even as a free agent.

Mostly, there was hope.

I picked up the phone, expecting to hear the voice of some scout or personnel guy, asking if I'd be interested in signing with his team. Interested? At that point, I would have walked across the country barefoot to go to someone's training camp.

Instead, what I heard was Amy's voice.

"Did anyone call yet?" she asked.

Hearts were dropping all over the house. I was so mad, I was ready to break up with her.

"Please don't call me here again tonight," I said, trying to keep my anger under control. "I promise I'll call you if I hear anything."

About ten or fifteen minutes later, the phone rang again. I was in the bathroom, so I didn't even hear it. I think someone made sure to pick up real fast, just in case it wasn't someone from an NFL team, so I wouldn't lose it again.

"Wayne John!" my mother said. "It's John Griffin."

"Who the heck is John Griffin and why is he calling here?"

The only John I was expecting to hear from at that point was Garrett. But this was John Griffin, the Jets' college scouting coordinator, and his call came as a complete shock to me.

"Hello?"

"Hi, Wayne. Did anybody call you yet?"

"No."

"Well, we're interested in you. We'd like to have you."

"That sounds good to me."

"We'll be getting in touch with your agent."

"Great."

And after I hung up, I was under the distinct impression

that that was it—the Jets were going to sign me as a free agent. I was going to get my shot.

I can't say the Jets were the team I had always dreamed of playing for, but I was still pretty excited. Although the last winning season they had had up to that point was in 1988, when they went 8–7–1, they still had the aura from that Broadway Joe Namath team that won Super Bowl III. Thirty years later, it continues to carry a lot of weight with the whole organization. We might have been a big Giants' family, but my parents had an oil painting of Namath hanging on the wall. (After being in storage for about fifteen years, that painting is proudly displayed again in my parents' home, only this time it has Joe Willie's autograph.)

After four years of staring across the Hempstead Turnpike at the Jets' training facility, I was finally going to know what it would be like to be one of those guys in the green and white uniforms.

Or at least, that was what I thought.

On the morning of Monday, April 24, I got another call. This one was from my agent. I was in my dorm room at Hofstra, and I figured Art would be telling me when to head over to the Jets' offices to sign the deal.

He wasn't.

He was calling to say that, while the Jets were interested in me, they weren't quite ready to sign me. Earlier, Art had gotten a call from Griffin asking him if he could get me to Hofstra for one more workout.

"Why?" Art said to him. "You know everything you need

to know about this guy. Why does he have to do another workout?"

"We want to take a look at Wayne one more time," Griffin said. "Can you get him out so the receivers coach can take a look at him?"

From what I could gather, John was pretty much in my corner. Being so close to Hofstra, he had had the chance to watch a lot of my games through the years. He was able to see a lot of the little things I could do—the blocking, the hustle, the aggressiveness—along with the big things, like the ability to catch the ball in traffic.

But he was out on a limb with me and he needed to get someone else in the Jets' organization, especially a higher-up, to share that opinion. The worst thing that can happen to one of these guys is to use up a spot on the roster for a player who turns out to be a bum. This is a competitive business, and not just at field level. Like players, personnel guys are looking to knock each other out of their spots all the time. Scouts want to become college scouting directors. College scouting directors want to become general managers.

"Look," Griffin said. "Would you just tell him it's important that he does this workout for us?"

"I'll call Wayne," Art said. "But I can't make any guarantees."

Little did I know that Art was telling Griffin that he had other NFL teams interested in me. There weren't any others, of course, but Art was desperate, trying to find any leverage he could find—even if it wasn't there. In fact, at one point, he said to him, "If you want him, you send the contract now and sign him."

The bluff didn't work. Griffin didn't have the authority to do anything but ask me to show up for another workout. The ultimate decision on whether I would be signed rested with Dick Haley, the Jets' director of player personnel.

So Art called me and said, "The Jets want to take one more look at you. Get your track shoes."

I couldn't believe it. After going through that meat market in Baltimore and all of those other workouts, after the disappointments from the Bengals and endless don't-call-us-we'll-call-you responses, this was not the kind of thing I was expecting.

I had sat through the draft. I had waited for what seemed like an eternity for an NFL team to call. Then, when one finally does, there is still another hoop for me to jump through?

"Do you think I should do it?" I asked Art.

"You know what, Wayne?" he said. "We've come this far. Why not give it one more go around?"

Along with my shorts and track shoes, I made sure to wear a tank top to my Jets' audition—just to show I was in good shape. It was one of those NO FEAR shirts that said: IT'S NOT THE SIZE OF THE DOG IN THE FIGHT; IT'S THE SIZE OF THE FIGHT IN THE DOG.

I guess it was my little way of reminding them that their final evaluation should not stop with how tall I was or how much I weighed or the fact I wasn't from Florida State.

The workout began around noon. Basically, it consisted of Richard Mann, the Jets' receivers coach at the time, firing balls at me while Haley and Griffin watched. Art was there, too. I noticed that later in the workout, the audience grew to include Jets assistant general manager James Harris, now director of pro personnel for the Baltimore Ravens, and Haley's son, Todd, who at the time was a scout for the team but is now part of the coaching staff.

I didn't have a choice but to catch every single pass. It was either catch them or go home. But that type of workout was right up my alley. To this day, I'm always ready to go out and have a catch. I'll do it anywhere, any time, with a football, a baseball, whatever.

After loosening up a little, Coach Mann, a pretty big guy who was forty-eight at the time, started throwing me the ball. We began about ten yards apart, and he was firing them all over. High. Low. To the side.

He put me through a comeback drill where I took one step forward, turned, and came sprinting toward him as he threw a bullet right at my face. There's a big difference between catching a ball this way as opposed to when you're running away from the passer. When you're running away from the passer, you have a little cushion as you pull the ball in and more time to adjust if necessary. But when you're running at him, the ball's going to hit your hands—if not a more sensitive part of your body—like a brick. If you don't catch that ball, you're either going to end up with a busted nose . . . or you're going to be singing funny.

At one point during the comeback drill, Coach Mann

turned to Haley and said, "This is what Jack Jackson couldn't do." Jackson, a University of Florida receiver who is about my size, apparently had problems making those comeback catches during a pre-draft workout.

There was one drill where I had my back to Coach Mann and I had to snap my body around while the ball was already in the air. Then I had to catch sideline passes while keeping my feet in bounds. Then I had to run a couple of routes.

But mostly it was just a matter of standing there, like I was in front of a firing squad.

This guy was out to break me, but I'm not the kind of guy that breaks. All I was thinking was, *Go ahead. Throw everything you've got at me. Give me more.*

I could have stayed out there all day.

After about forty-five minutes, Coach Mann stopped throwing passes, so I stopped running routes. The workout was over.

Then Coach Mann walked up to me and, in a quiet voice, said, "Hey, good job. You're strong enough, you're fast enough, you can make all the catches. I'm pulling for you."

But I still didn't see any papers for me to sign. There still wasn't anyone uttering those magic words: "Congratulations, Wayne. You're a New York Jet!"

Instead, what Art and I heard from Haley was: "What else have you got going on?"

"Well, I was supposed to get back to the Saints by four o'clock," Art said.

Although Art had had some conversations with the Saints, there was no real hope that they were going to offer me a contract. In fact, that morning Art had spoken by phone with Tom Marino, a Saints scout, and had been told that if there was any interest from another club, we should pursue it. Otherwise, if Art felt like calling Tom at four, he could. But Tom certainly wasn't going to be anxiously awaiting his call.

Then Haley said, "We'll get back to you in a couple of hours."

We were stunned and disappointed.

I had caught every ball there. And I do mean every ball—the ones that were barely an inch off the ground and the ones that sailed as far over my head as I could reach. And the best they could do was tell me that they'd get back to me in a couple of hours?

Before I walked off the field, I expected to know—one way or another—the outcome of that workout. I figured they might talk it over for a few minutes, then tell me their decision. And if they said no, the one positive that would have come out of that was that I could say to myself, *I'm just not good enough. Because I know I've done my best. It wasn't an off day. I did everything I possibly could to convince them that I deserve a chance, and they just didn't see it. It's just not there.*

But I never thought they were going to say, "We'll get back to you in a couple of hours." I never thought we were *still* going to be left hanging.

This was how Art would later describe the look on my face: "It was a look that said: 'How hard do you want me to punch him? Do I punch him to kill him on the spot or do I just maim him?'"

What could we do? What could we say that was going to

change anything? It wasn't like there were scouts from other teams waiting in the wings, ready to grab me if the Jets didn't.

Still, Art decided to give it his best shot.

"Hey, you've got to make a decision right now," he said to Haley with a little bit of an edge to his voice. "We're going back to Wayne's dorm to wait for an answer, but I told the Saints I'd get back to them by four o'clock. And to be honest with you, if you guys aren't back to us by four o'clock, this train's leaving the station."

In truth, the Saints were nothing more than a dim hope and we had nothing going on with any other team.

At first, I gave Art a look that said, *What the hell are you talking about?*

Then, under his breath, he told me to start walking away with him and to keep my head up, like I knew that there would be something else available for me if the Jets didn't give me a contract—which we both knew was total BS.

My attitude was: *Do what you have to do, Art. Don't worry that my whole life is in your hands.*

We got back to my dorm, on the second floor of Dover House in Colonial Square East. Amy met us there. We had started dating a year earlier. And even though this whole NFL auditioning thing wasn't something we even thought about when we first started going out, now that I had gone through it, I'd be lying if I said I wasn't trying to impress her a little bit. So being left up in the air by the Jets was just making things worse.

I didn't tell too many people about the workout, but those who did know about it, such as my suitemates, Brian and Pat, couldn't wait to ask, "What happened?"

I just said, "Don't ask me that."

Then I started to let off some steam, throwing shirts and towels everywhere. I knew that all I was really doing was making a messy room messier, but it made me feel better.

"I can't believe this," I yelled. "I've never caught the ball like I caught it today. And there's still a doubt? If I was six-foot-two, they would sign me in a minute."

Art tried to calm me down.

"It's all right," he said. "It will happen. You're OK. Something is going to work out here. I've got to tell you something: Human beings can't catch footballs any better than you just did out there. And they know it."

Part of me wanted to believe him. Part of me just figured he was trying to make me feel better.

Finally, right around four o'clock, the phone rang. Art picked it up. It was Dick Haley.

"OK, we want to sign him," he said. "Why don't you come over?"

At this point, Art must have figured he was on a roll because the next thing out of his mouth was: "Hey, Dick. Wayne needs a little money up-front."

"I don't know about that," Haley said. "We're offering him an opportunity here . . ."

"Come on," Art said. "All he wants is twenty-five hundred dollars. You know that's the going rate for an undrafted guy in this league."

147

Haley hemmed and hawed for a minute, then said, "How about fifteen hundred?"

"You've got a deal."

I was just happy to know I'd be getting a standard rookie contract for the then-league minimum of one hundred and nineteen thousand dollars a year. Of course, I wasn't going to see a nickel of that money unless I made the team. And I would have to stay on the roster for the full sixteen-game regular season to see it all.

On the other hand, the signing bonus would be paid immediately. Do you know how many nickel beers you can buy for fifteen hundred bucks? Up to that point, most of the spending money I had came from whatever my father gave me on my weekend trips home. Amy and I would roll pennies and quarters just to go to the movies.

I shook hands with Art. I gave Amy a big kiss. At that moment, it dawned on us that it had really happened—that after all we had been through, I was finally going to get my shot. I had finally kicked down that door to the NFL.

We headed across the turnpike to Weeb Ewbank Hall. It might have been a short drive, but it felt like we were landing on the moon. But wait. There was one more obstacle: The secretaries had already gone home, so I wouldn't be able to sign the actual papers until the next day, Tuesday, April 25.

Art and I hung around for about fifteen minutes, making arrangements to come back the next day and sign the contract. Just before we left, Art told Haley, "You may not realize it now, but the guy you're going to sign will always be one of the best receivers—if not the best receiver—on this team."

Now I'm the kind of guy who doesn't believe any transaction is complete unless it is legally in writing. I don't trust many things. I don't believe in promises—except those from Mom, Dad, and Jen. If anyone else promises me something, I usually expect it *not* to happen.

It's not that I expect bad things to happen to me, but if you don't expect a lot, you won't be let down as much. The way I look at it, it's not the job of other people to make my life euphoric; it's up to me.

That whole night I was thinking, *There's still a chance something could go wrong. They could change their minds in the morning. Dick Haley could wake up and say, "You know, I think we're all wrong about Chrebet. That kid isn't worth fifteen hundred dollars. Hell, he isn't worth fifteen cents."*

Or maybe he'll just forget my name altogether.

When Art and I returned to Weeb Ewbank Hall the next morning, the contract was ready for me to sign . . . but not before I made a radical change in headgear. I was wearing my Giants cap. I didn't even think about it being inappropriate because the Giants had always been my team and that was the hat I usually wore. But the Jets did. Haley and the other front-office types that met with us didn't appreciate seeing the enemy's colors in *their* training complex and, right away, they gave me a Jets hat.

The next stop was to see James Harris to sign the contract. After a quick review of the paperwork by Art, I put my name on the dotted line and I was, at long last, a Jet.

Our final meeting of the day was with Richard Mann, who would be my position coach. And the first thing Coach Mann, who is black, said was: "I don't coach color. If you can play, you can play . . . or you are going to be out of here."

I respected him for saying that.

Maybe because of the hat thing and the fact that I had just put my name on a piece of paper that seemed to say as much, I started to feel like I was part of the Jets' family. So I got up the nerve to ask for an official NFL football to take with me, so I could maybe do a little working out on my own before mini-camp, which would begin a few days later, or to just toss it around in my dorm room.

My feeling couldn't have been more off the mark because they wouldn't give it to me. I guess they figured, with the fifteen hundred dollars they had just put in my pocket, I could buy two or three footballs of my own.

As far as I was concerned, getting that contract would be harder than actually making the team. At least I knew I had some control over making the team.

If I got the chance and didn't make it, I only had myself to blame.

10

"You're Not Supposed to Be Here"

I knew what it would take for me to make the Jets' final roster. It would take a whole summer's worth of performances like the one I gave during that workout.

Every pass route would have to be run to perfection. Every ball would have to be caught. Every practice would have to be more productive than the one before.

Being a fan, I had never seen a lot of free agents make any

team in the NFL. The ones that did had something in common: They didn't screw up very often.

I just needed to get that first step through the door. That's what I was concentrating on. If I could just do that, I knew I could take care of the rest.

I expected to face obstacles, such as cornerbacks that glued themselves to me . . . and quarterbacks that sometimes wouldn't throw the ball anywhere near where I was running . . . and a playbook the size of the Manhattan telephone directory to learn.

I just never dreamed that the first obstacle was going to be Harry Fisher. Harry was not a cornerback, a quarterback, or a coach. He was the security guard at the Jets' training complex.

And when I showed up for my first minicamp, on April 28, 1995, Harry wouldn't let me through the fence.

As if it weren't already obvious enough that most guys my size watch pro football rather than play it, Harry made certain to add one more reminder: He thought I was some kid trying to get autographs.

Now you have to know a little background on Harry. He was about seventy years old at the time. He stood around five-foot-seven, with a big belly that hung over his pants. He also was the only Jet security guard who wore a full uniform, complete with a ranger hat that made him look like John Candy as the security guard at Wally World. (About a year later, I would find out that the Jets didn't even make him wear the uniform; he just wanted to because he was so gung-ho about his job.)

Harry had this really scratchy voice and he tried to sound like the toughest, meanest SOB around, but he was actually a teddy bear. He would talk your ear off about any subject. Amy told me that while she was waiting for me after practice one day, Harry spent about fifteen minutes talking about his method for taking a shower every morning (not a pretty sight, I'm sure), explaining how he turned the water on a certain way to get the temperature just right. He would go on and on, and it would always crack me up.

Harry was a great guy. We had a lot of laughs, right up through his retirement after the 1997 season.

Of course, on that first day of minicamp, I thought Harry was being a real jerk.

"You don't understand," I said. "I play for the Jets."

"Sure you do, son," Harry said. "Now run along. You're not supposed to be here."

Besides not being as tall as your average NFL player, I guess it also didn't help that I was carrying a backpack with my books in it because I had just come from a class at Hofstra. And I suppose I did nothing to diminish Harry's suspicion by pulling into the parking lot in my little Isuzu pickup truck. "Real" players zip into the place in BMWs, Mercedes, and Lexuses. And the ones that drive trucks have big, shiny, top-of-the-line sport utility vehicles, not little pickups.

"No, I really am part of the team," I kept saying to Harry. "Really!"

"Yeah, yeah, son," Harry said. "Now you're going to have to leave."

I wasn't going anywhere, of course. Not until I got in uniform, got on the field, and got the chance to show the coaches what I could do. If, after that, they wanted to throw me out of there, fine. Maybe signing a contract as a lowly free agent didn't entitle you to a ball, but it was supposed to allow you to participate in at least one minicamp practice.

I kept my cool, though. I wasn't looking for trouble. I certainly didn't want to scrap with old Harry. I would have if I had to, but I didn't think it would look too good for a rookie player, on his first day with the team, to be trading punches with the security guard. Couldn't you just see the headline in the next day's *New York Post?* PUNK ROOKIE NO-NAME DUKES IT OUT WITH VETERAN JETS' SECURITY GUARD!

Finally someone else who worked for the team saw me standing outside and waved me through.

When Harry saw that, he immediately became apologetic.

"Oh, I'm sorry," he said. "I really am."

Every time I saw Harry after that, we laughed about his honest mistake. Until his retirement, he kind of kept it going as a running joke, always asking me who I was when I showed up for practice. And I'd always tell him I was just a kid looking for autographs.

At the time, though, it was just another reminder of the task ahead of me—another indication of just how high the odds were stacked against me.

• • •

Minicamps aren't the greatest barometer to gauge whether or not a player truly belongs in the NFL. There are no pads; there is no contact.

It's basically three days of orientation, mostly for the sake of the younger guys. You meet with your position coaches, get a quick rundown of all your plays, and then, with your head spinning out of control, you hit the field and pray that you don't mess up too bad.

Most of the veterans hate minicamp. They'd rather be anywhere else, preferably holding a golf club. But it means everything in the world to a rookie—especially a long shot free agent that almost no one aside from Harry Fisher even knew was there.

I was counting down the hours, minutes, and seconds until I could get on that field for the very first time. I had to take advantage of every moment that I was on display before Rich Kotite—in his first year as the Jets' head coach after five seasons with the Philadelphia Eagles—and his assistants. I knew those moments would be few and far between because there were ten wide receivers on the depth chart. And I was tenth.

You had the starters, a couple of second-year guys named Ryan Yarborough and Stevie Anderson, who were getting the first crack at taking over for Rob Moore, who had been traded to Arizona, and one of the game's all-time greats, Art Monk, who was not re-signed.

You had Orlando Parker, another second-year player, in the third spot, followed by two first-year guys: Alan Allen, who had led the World League in receptions, and Tom Garlick from Fordham. You had two draft choices: Tyrone Davis, a fourth-rounder from Virginia, and Curtis Ceaser (we called him "Julius"), a seventh-rounder from Grambling. You had the other rookie free agents—Chad Askew from Pittsburgh and Brian Sallee from Missouri.

Then came good old Wayne Whathisname from Whatchamacallit University.

In college, I had gotten so used to being a big fish in a small pond. Now I felt like a microorganism in the ocean. It's unbelievable how far you can fall before you actually start the climb. That is, if you start to climb at all.

Even my uniform number, 3, was bottom-of-the-totem-pole stuff. I thought I would get something in the 80s or teens, the usual numbers for NFL receivers, but all of them were taken. One of the equipment guys finally said, "Just pick a number."

I don't think he thought I was going to be around long enough for it to make a difference anyway.

The circumstances were so much different when I chose 3 at Hofstra. In my sophomore year, I got together with two of my good friends and teammates—Jeff Bechetti and Jon Camera, a quarterback who decided to play baseball at Hofstra instead of football—and we decided to take numbers 1, 2, and 3.

That was fine for college. But when you see a small white guy with a single-digit number in the NFL, you don't think "receiver." You think "kicker." I felt like one of the Zendejas brothers.

Of course, if I had to, I would have worn 106½. It didn't matter to me. The only thing I cared about was making the team.

I have to admit, it was a little overwhelming the first time I got into the huddle with Boomer Esiason. I was in sixth grade when he began his quarterbacking career with the Bengals in 1984. Then I looked over and there was Johnny Mitchell, the tight end. I was in my second year at Hofstra, glued to the TV set when the Jets plucked him from Nebraska with the fifteenth overall pick of the 1992 draft.

It was like, *What the heck am I doing here?*

It's a little difficult to feel like you belong on an NFL team when you're still going to college classes at the same place you're participating in a minicamp. While all of the other rookies and out-of-town players stayed across the street at the Long Island Marriott, I stayed in my dorm room.

During those three months before training camp, I was running every day like a maniac in Wanaque. To gauge the kind of shape I was in, I used to have races with Luke, the first of our two golden retrievers. We'd go over to one end of our street, I'd yell, "Go!", and Luke would know exactly what to do—try to get to the house before I did. I beat him every time, but the key was the margin of victory. If it was by several feet, I knew I was in top condition. If it was only by a couple of steps, I knew I had more work to do.

I didn't think my height would be any more of a problem

for me in the NFL than it was in college, but I knew how I would be perceived at the next level—as being too small to cut it. I couldn't control my height, even if I hung from a swing set like Bobby Brady of "The Brady Bunch" when he tried to make himself taller.

I couldn't control what anyone thought about my height, either.

Therefore, I concentrated on everything that I could control like getting faster, getting quicker, running better routes, catching the ball better. I worked on all of those things to compensate for whatever the Jets' coaches thought I might have lacked. Not only compensate, but overcompensate.

We were given sheets containing the plays we would run in minicamp and had to learn by the time training camp opened in July. We couldn't take the playbook home, but we could take those sheets. The receivers had only about twenty plays, with different formations for each one, but I made a point of knowing them inside out. I studied them during the day, at night, even when I was on the beach.

When I got to camp, I just wanted to worry about performing, not trying to learn the plays. I would still have to learn the complex defensive schemes that you see in the NFL, which would take some time. But knowing those twenty plays was a great start.

I was smart enough to learn both sides of the playbook. So if someone got hurt at any of the receiver positions—X, Y, or Z—I could fill right in. Hell, I would have studied the running plays if they would have let me.

I believed in a very simple principle: The more you can do, the less reason they have to cut you.

I think most people who knew I had signed with the Jets figured the first time I would lose some blood would be the first time we started popping the pads in training camp. Being Wayne "Accident" Chrebet, I couldn't wait that long, of course.

About a week before camp opened, I got together with Dave Saper, one of my closest friends from college, to play some pickup basketball in the gym of a health club in Paramus called Spa Two. I was there for the first time in my life, going as Dave's guest.

We played half-court games where you kept playing until you lost. Naturally, I didn't want to lose. I didn't want to get off that court. Regardless of the game or where it's being played, I play to win. And on that day, I was competing as if we were in Game Seven of the NBA Finals.

All of a sudden, a guy I wasn't covering from the other team went dribbling past me. Following my natural instincts, I went running full speed behind him to take the ball away. At the last second, he decided to turn, his teeth collided with my forehead, and he dropped to the floor.

Because the gym was also where the Spa held its aerobic classes, mirrors surrounded it. I looked at my reflection and saw blood dripping down my forehead and streaming down my nose. Not that it mattered to the guy who had done the damage. He started yelling at me because my skull caused him to lose a tooth.

"Hey, it was an accident," I said. "I wasn't trying to hurt myself, either."

The guy didn't seem interested in my point of view. He just kept on yelling about his missing tooth.

"Look, pal, if you keep this up, I'm going to knock the rest of your teeth out for real," I said. "Now relax. It was an accident."

He finally calmed down, but my cut sure didn't. Butterfly Band-Aids couldn't close it. So the next day Tim Gray, my good friend from Wanaque, drove me to the emergency room to get the gash in my forehead stitched up.

I was so embarrassed by the thought of reporting to my first NFL training camp looking like Frankenstein that I had my father, the former Army medic, take out the stitches just before I left for Hempstead. I felt like Rocky, sitting on the stool with that big welt over his eye, saying, "Cut me, Mick."

Dad did a great job. You could hardly tell the stitches were ever in there. Of all of the ways I wanted to gain attention that summer, an accident in a pickup basketball game wasn't one of them. In fact, I would have been happy if no one gave me a second look until I was on the practice field, even though that went directly against the advice I had been given from someone—I don't remember who—from Hofstra. He told me that in order to get noticed in an NFL camp, there should be something different about you, something that sets you apart from everyone else. Whether that meant shaving your head or having some sort of weird ritual or goofy dance, he said you should do something that makes everyone notice you, something that makes you stand out.

I appreciated the fact he was trying to be helpful, but I'm not much for hooting or hollering or making any sort of fashion statement. I decided the best way I could stand out was by catching every damn ball thrown to me—no matter how, no matter where.

I had to be able to go long. I had to be able to go short. And most of all, I had to be able to go across the middle, make the catch, get drilled, get up, and act like nothing ever happened. I was going to show the coaches my toughness. I was going to show them that I could be counted on every down, every distance.

That's something I have always lived by.

I had to know, right away, if it was going to be possible to make that mammoth jump from Hofstra to the NFL.

That was why, for my first one-on-one drill, I picked out the best cornerback I could face—Pro Bowler Aaron Glenn. I watched where Aaron wound up on the line of cornerbacks that formed across from the line of receivers. By letting someone move ahead of me and jumping behind someone else, I made certain we were in the same spot of our respective lines and, therefore, would go against each other.

As we both stepped up for that first showdown, waiting for Boomer to take the snap, I thought to myself, *I've really got to do something to not only impress the coaches, but to gain the respect of Aaron and the other DBs. If the people I go up against every day in practice don't think much of my ability as a player, no one else on the team will, either.*

I decided to run a deep route, which would be the last thing anyone would think I would do because of Aaron's great speed and one-on-one coverage skills. The expectation was that I would run something shorter, like a slant, a quick out, a regular out, or an in route—anything that would give me the best chance of catching the ball.

Boomer took the snap and Aaron and I took off together. I gave him a little head-and-shoulder fake, like I was running a short pattern. Aaron got turned around and I just took off deep. All of a sudden, there I was, running down the sideline by myself to catch Boomer's perfectly thrown pass.

All right, I said to myself. *If I can do something like that against a player of Aaron's caliber, then I think I can play in this league.* I saw the mountain. I just wanted to know if it was climbable, and it was . . . even if the top still looked a hundred miles away.

The next day a TV interviewer asked me, "What do you think the odds are of you making the team?"

I thought about it for a second.

"I'm not going to say whether I think I'm going to make it or not," I said. "But let's put it this way: When I came over the Throgs Neck Bridge on my way over here, I didn't buy a round-trip token."

That didn't change the fact that I was the consummate long shot. In fact, it wasn't long before Boomer and a lot of others on and off the team began calling me "Rudy," as in Daniel "Rudy" Ruettiger, who became a national symbol for long shots when he made a dream come true by playing football for Notre Dame in the final seconds of the final game of his senior year. (Although I thought of myself as having more athletic talent than the real Rudy, I was inspired by the movie about his life. I also liked the name enough to give it to the second golden retriever my parents got later that year.)

One of the great things about practicing at my alma mater was the support I had not only from my family—my parents made the trip from New Jersey almost every day and Jen often took the train from Manhattan to catch our afternoon workout—but also from a lot of fans. Anytime I'd make a catch, about two hundred people would applaud and shout, "Go, Hofstra!" With each day, I noticed that I was becoming a little bit more of a fan favorite, and it felt good.

It didn't take long for me to figure out that, as a rookie, the amount of practice or playing time you get depends on where you come from. If you're a high draft pick, you can take your sweet time showing the coaches what you can do because with the big signing bonus that has been invested in you, you're going to stick around for a while. If you come in as a rookie free agent, the coaches need to see results. Immediately!

I have seen guys in camp that I thought could play in this league, but they never got a chance to really show their stuff. And when you don't get a chance with one team, why should another bother to try you out?

The other thing you hear—over and over—from coaches

and players is: "You can't make the club in the tub." In other words, every day that you're injured and not practicing, your chances of making the team are like the old snowball in hell, melting away by the second. I took that saying to heart. I still do. As long as all of my limbs are in one piece and I'm conscious—or at least, semiconscious—I'm going to practice and play.

I got hurt pretty bad one day in that first training camp. I caught a bomb and came down on my right shoulder hard, with the defender landing on top of me. My shoulder was killing me, but I did everything I could to keep anyone else from knowing about it. I would get a bag of ice and carry on, not telling or showing anyone what it was for. Then, whenever I was alone in my dorm room, I would put the ice on my shoulder and keep it there until it was time to go to practice or a meeting.

The pain never really went away and was downright excruciating at times. But I sure as hell wasn't about to watch from the sidelines. I had such tunnel vision. There was no alternative to being on the field. It didn't matter what happened, I was going to be out there. Besides, it's hard enough getting anyone to notice you when you have to wait for nine other guys to take their reps. There would be days when I would only got one rep through an entire practice.

Slowly but surely, though, nature takes its course. One day someone pulls a hamstring and is out of the rotation. Then another guy twists a knee. Then a third guy falls out of favor with the coaches for making too many mistakes or not showing enough hustle.

The next thing you know, I'm in for a couple of extra reps.

I tried to make the most of every opportunity. For a guy with my background, it wasn't enough to be just ordinary. I had to do spectacular things, like the day I made a lunging grab on a bomb from Glenn Foley, then a short while later turned cornerback Carl Greenwood, our fifth-round pick, inside out on a corner route.

When you do something special, like make a diving catch, the coaches ask, "Hey, can you do that again?" And boom! You have three more chances.

It seemed like that was happening to me every other practice. A diving catch here. A leaping catch there. A whole bunch of short routes that turned into long gains. And very few dropped passes or patterns run the wrong way.

All of a sudden, I'm moving up the depth chart. I go from the tenth spot to the sixth spot. Then to the fourth spot. Then, when we go to three wides, I'm in there as the third receiver.

For most of that summer, I took the approach that I would let my actions do most of my talking and speak only when spoken to. I stayed away from the head coach, and I stayed away from a lot of teammates.

I don't know if people thought something was wrong with me—if I was crazy or what. But that was the way I approached it. I was just there to play. To me, it was a job interview. It was an audition. It was business.

I respected everyone there, I was nice to everybody, but I

wasn't looking to make any friends yet. So most of the time, I would just sit there in meetings, with my baseball cap pulled down over my eyes, and not say a word. I'd just sit there and listen to people.

I wasn't really shy or intimidated. Let's just say I was focused.

In training camp, like boot camp, the idea is to train your mind as well as your body. And the first thing your mind learns to do is worry. Worry about knowing the plays. Worry about getting to the right spot on the field. Worry about catching the ball. Worry about being on time for every meeting and every ankle-taping and every practice.

The routine is enough to make you a little crazy. You wake up early in the morning, eat breakfast, practice, eat lunch, try to take a nap, practice again. Then, after about an hour and a half, you go to a meeting with your position coach until nine-thirty at night.

You come back to your dorm, exhausted. You have nothing else to think about except trying to make the team. You don't see a female for so long that you start looking at each other funny.

There are days at practice when you see guys doing things and say to yourself, *I know I can do that just as well—if not better.* Then there are nights when you're lying in bed thinking, *This is not going to happen . . . This is the worst experience of my life . . . I just want to go home.*

All NFL rookies go though a certain amount of hazing, although I didn't get it quite as bad as Kyle Brady did. He was the number-one pick, so the veterans made him sing the Penn State fight song in the dining hall all of the time. They made me to sing, too, but not nearly as often.

I never got the sense that any of the other players really disrespected me, although you could see in some of their faces that they didn't think I belonged there at first. Until I put on my helmet one day, Matt Willig, one of our offensive tackles, swore I was a ball boy or some kid who had sneaked into the locker room to get an autograph.

With my focused approach to practice, I think I made it clear right away that I wasn't just looking to tell my college buddies that I got to spend three weeks on the Jets' eighty-man camp roster. I was there to compete for a job.

And the more reps I had in practice, the more I began to feel accepted by the other players. I began to feel more a part of the team, especially when I was around Boomer. He came up with all sorts of nicknames for me. Once I dispelled the notion that I was another "Rudy," Boomer changed my nickname to "Nails," because he thought I showed the same kind of toughness Lenny "Nails" Dykstra displayed as a center fielder on World Series teams with the Mets and Phillies.

But Boomer's most lasting nickname was "Q," which came from one of the many mispronunciations of my name. Apparently, on the first day of practice, Boomer had asked an assistant coach who I was. The coach replied, "I think his name is Quebert."

Just about everyone on the team has called me "Q" ever since.

Boomer treated me great. I wasn't in there as a cocky rookie. He saw what I was trying to do, how hard I was working to beat the odds and make the team, and I think he appreciated that.

Because there were no veteran receivers in camp to show me the ropes, Boomer kind of took me under his wing. He let me pick his brain, and I never hesitated to take advantage of that. I constantly asked him questions like: "What are you reading on this play? Are you looking my way first? What do you want me to do on my route? Do you want me to come across slow, so you can read the field as you're dropping back and setting up in the pocket? Do you want me to come across fast, so you can throw to me quick?"

He would patiently answer everything, trying to provide as much information as he could to help make me a better receiver.

Boomer is probably the best student of the game that I know. He's amazing. He could tell you everything that is going on on the field. It wasn't so much that he saw things other people didn't see. It was that he saw them quicker. He picked up all of the tendencies, the blitzes, the coverages. He was very thorough. That served him well as a quarterback and will keep serving him well as an analyst for ABC's "Monday Night Football."

Catching Boomer's left-handed passes was a little bit different than catching all of the ones thrown to me through the years by right-handers. I guess the best way to describe it would be that instead of the point of the ball traveling northeast when it got to your hands, it was northwest. I spent a lot of extra time working with Boomer in practice, so that eventually, catching those lefty deliveries became second nature.

During camp, Boomer said this about me to reporters: "He's taken the attitude of an underdog and molded himself into a pretty damn good little football player. In this day and age, to be honest with you, it's refreshing to see a young athlete work his butt off to make the team. He's been given an opportunity and he's making the most of it. It's a nice story and hopefully that story will continue as the season goes on."

Whether he really meant it or was just being kind, those words meant a lot to me. It was something I needed to hear as a rookie just trying to survive practice to practice and drill to drill.

We had yet to begin our preseason schedule, which would serve as the acid test of whether I had what it took to stick. To make a lasting impact, I knew I was going to have to come up big against someone without the word "Jets" on his helmet.

"I think he's looked good in drills, but he has to carry it over to a game situation," Coach Mann told a reporter about me. "One on one, he's made some plays. He's been a pleasant surprise early. But I haven't seen him under the gun to judge him fully yet."

Our first preseason game was at Tampa Bay. I never got to play one snap at receiver in our 9–3 victory. I just got three plays as a gunner on special teams. It was a fairly new role for me, and I didn't do anything spectacular. The one time I got down the field first, I whiffed completely on the tackle. I didn't even come close.

Coach Mann promised me that I'd get to play receiver in our second game, against Philadelphia. But I didn't put a whole lot of stock into something like that. I knew I could just as easily have been cut the day after we got back from Tampa. Rookies who see little or no playing time in the preseason are usually the first to get a visit from The Turk. That's what we called Mike Kensil, the Jets' director of operations whose duty it was to inform players when they were cut.

The veterans make sure you know all about The Turk. They scare the hell out of you, saying things like: "If this guy knocks on your door, you'd better watch out. Because when The Turk comes calling, it's all over for you."

The Turk didn't come calling for me that week.

We faced the Eagles in Jackson, Mississippi. I watched the first three quarters from the sidelines in my nice clean uniform. Finally, in the fourth quarter, I got inserted at receiver.

I went up against cornerback Bobby Taylor, a highly regarded second-round draft pick that year from Notre Dame. In our first series, I caught two balls on him. Taylor was all over me on the first one, but I still managed to haul it in. Later, I drew a pass interference penalty, closing out what I felt was a pretty productive debut at receiver—three catches for twenty-five yards—for the amount of time I played.

Even though it was the fourth quarter and most of the least experienced players were on the field, I did something positive. And that meant I would stick around for another week. When you do something positive in a preseason game, it doesn't necessarily mean that you'll make the team. It just gives you another week's pass to prove that what you did was no fluke and maybe show that you can do even better the next time.

Two days later in practice, I found myself getting some work with the first unit. I tried not to read too much into that because a lot of times, coaches will change around the starters to motivate other players. I really didn't think I was in the starting lineup to stay.

Our third preseason game was the one my whole family and all of our friends and relatives prayed I would be around for. It was against the Giants at Giants Stadium. I was facing the team I had admired for so many years and I still admire. Before that night, I had only been in the place as a fan—a Giants' fan—and I had never set foot on the field.

There were a couple of hundred people in the stands that I knew had come just to see me get some action, even if only for a few plays. They were all there . . . my parents, my sister, my uncles, aunts, cousins, girlfriend, friends from college, friends from high school, friends from growing up, coaches from high school, teachers from high school.

And there were so many other people there that I didn't know but who also were on hand to see me in action. I think most of the city of Garfield showed up.

Having that many familiar eyes staring at you creates a tremendous amount of pressure. But I wouldn't have wanted it any other way. I like to do things that bring cheers from the people I know and love. Other guys might say, "This is too much. I can't handle it. I'm afraid I'll screw up." Not me. My attitude is: *Bring more. Fill the whole stadium with people I know.* To me, that's a treat.

I was thinking, *This is the highlight of my career. This is the Super Bowl of my life.*

All of a sudden, at the end of the first quarter, I hear Kotite, in that deep, tough-sounding voice of his, yell, "Chevette! Chevette! Get in there!"

At first, I didn't know who he was talking to because until that point he had only referred to me as "Number Three." Now I couldn't tell if he wanted me in the game or was asking someone to bring his car up from valet parking.

I thought it was pretty early for me to go in there because a lot of the starters were still in the game. But a couple of receivers had gotten hurt and Tyrone Davis, one of the rookies who were ahead of me on the depth chart, was winded.

Finally I said to myself, *The hell with it. Chevette is close enough to Chrebet. I'm going in.* Although I ended up catching only one pass in our 32–31 loss—a twelve-yard reception on third-and-six—I showed the whole time I was in there that I could consistently get open and block well.

Two days later, as all NFL teams trimmed their rosters to sixty, The Turk made a whole bunch of visits to the player dorms. Among the players cut were three receivers—Stevie, Tom, and Orlando.

With Askew having torn up his knee early on and Sallee getting cut before the first preseason game, that left five receivers on the roster: Ryan, Tyrone, Curtis, Alan, and me. Between us, we had a grand total of six NFL receptions, all by Yarborough. There was plenty of speculation all over the place that a trade would soon be made for a veteran receiver, meaning none of us could feel safe.

I got one of the biggest scares of my life the morning those cuts came down.

In the dorm I was in, there was a door that opened up to a little foyer, then two doors side by side leading to separate rooms. I had one and John Sacca, a rookie quarterback from Eastern Kentucky, had the other. I am a really deep sleeper. It usually takes a nuclear blast to wake me up.

But at exactly 6:50 A.M., I heard a knock on what I thought was my door. I sat right up in bed, figuring it was The Turk. I thought, *Jesus! This is like death coming to get you.*

Then I heard the other door open up. The Turk was there for John. I couldn't hear their conversation, but I didn't have to. John was the fourth quarterback, and no team keeps more than three on the active roster.

I kept waiting to see if The Turk was going to knock on my door, too. But when I heard the door to the foyer close, I knew The Turk was gone. I let out a giant exhale, then collapsed on my pillow.

I had set my alarm for eight o'clock, an hour before a

brief team meeting, which would be followed by a special teams meeting. After months of agonizing, I was in such a state of relaxation that I must have slipped into a coma because I slept right through the alarm. When I finally woke up, the radio was blaring in my ear. It was after nine. The team meeting was already over, the special teams meeting had started . . . and I was on the opposite side of the campus from where I was supposed to be at that very moment.

I almost had a heart attack.

I just popped my contacts in my eyes, grabbed my playbook, and started flying to the special teams meeting in a panic. The whole way over I'm thinking, *OK, they didn't cut me a couple of hours ago, but they're going to cut me now.*

I sprinted up the stairs. Then, just before I opened the door to where the meeting was being held, I kind of caught my breath and calmed myself just enough so I wouldn't be going in there like a maniac. At that point, I was a good ten to fifteen minutes late for Ken Rose's special teams meeting, which is more than enough to get you into serious trouble. Thirty seconds is enough.

The meeting was in a big auditorium. The lights were on. Everyone could see you going in or coming out. There was no way to just slip inside inconspicuously. But I decided that, rather than make any commotion over the fact I was late, I would walk in as conspicuously as possible. I acted like I hadn't missed a beat, like I was late because Rich or my position coach needed to see me about something after the team meeting—the team meeting I had never attended. I just walked in like: *Hey, I'm here, no problem. Why would I be late without a good reason?*

Of course, inside I was dying. I figured my heart would explode at any second.

I was also waiting for Ken to start tearing into me for showing up so late and disrupting his meeting. But I sat down and Ken kept on coaching without saying a thing to me. I didn't even get fined.

As I said, I felt no real comfort in being one of the five surviving receivers at that point. The Jets were still supposedly trying to make a trade, and names like Victor Bailey and Willie Davis of Kansas City, Shawn Jefferson of San Diego, Ernie Mills of Pittsburgh, and Michael Jackson of Cleveland were being mentioned in the media as possibilities. There was also the option of picking up a more experienced receiver who would be cut from another team.

Randy Lange of the *Bergen Record* wrote that while I was still in the hunt to make the final roster, a more likely spot for me was on the practice squad.

"I wouldn't be disappointed about that," I told him. "Sure, I'd like to be a part of the active squad, but the practice squad would also be a stepping-stone for me. When I first came out, I don't think anybody expected me to get this far."

The fourth and final preseason game was at Cincinnati. I got a huge surprise right before kickoff when I found out I would be starting opposite Yarborough. I must have had a pretty worried look on my face in the locker room before the game because Rich came up to me and said, "Just pretend you're about to play on the other side of the Hempstead Turnpike."

I only played the first quarter of our 30–24 victory. But it was the biggest and best quarter of my pro football life at that point.

I had five catches for fifty-four yards. And I made some decent plays. On our first drive, Boomer threw a pass to me over the middle. While spinning, I tipped the ball three times, kept my concentration, and made the catch in traffic. Later, I caught a short pass from Boomer near the sideline and made an inside spin on cornerback Roger Jones to pick up an extra fifteen yards. That was a move I made a million times at Hofstra.

Then Rich took me out. I wanted to stay on the field forever, of course. But then I thought, *Being taken out now has got to be a good thing. I put in a good performance. Now I don't have to worry about taking away from it by dropping a ball or running a bad route or getting hurt.*

It was the perfect ending to a perfect night.

Up in the stands, my father and mother were going nuts. My dad was on his cell phone, calling Art in New Jersey to give him a blow-by-blow description of what I was doing.

I considered that game my true test of the preseason. I knew the questions going through Rich's mind: *How is this guy going to react to being a starter? Can he perform under this pressure? Can he hold his own going a whole quarter against another team's starters?*

When he pulled me out, that meant—basically—I had passed the test.

I also looked at that game like this: The Bengals were the team that told me they were going to draft me or sign me to a free agent contract, and they did neither. I wanted to show them what they were missing.

I think I did.

11

Catching a Dream

In the locker room after the Cincinnati game, Bill Hampton, the Jets' longtime equipment manager, asked me, "What number do you want? We've got 80 . . . 83 . . . 85. Take your choice."

I couldn't believe it. I was being offered a real receivers' number. No more single-digit kickers' stuff. No more Wayne Zendejas. I thought, *This must be a good sign.*

But with seven more cuts to go to get the roster at the

regular-season limit of fifty-three—and continued talk that a trade was in the works for a veteran receiver—I wasn't ready to believe I had anything made yet.

I picked 80 because it was the number of some of the greatest receivers ever to play the game. I have never really been one to be in awe of athletes, but I have always had the utmost respect and admiration for two players who made that number famous—Jerry Rice, who is on his way to the Pro Football Hall of Fame, and Steve Largent, who is already there.

I didn't have a real understanding of the game when I first started watching those guys play—Rice for San Francisco and Largent for Seattle. But in their later years, when I understood the game better, I had a much greater appreciation for what they did—for the tremendous amount of work they put into their training and preparation even after reaching the very top of their profession, for the precise way they would run their patterns and make their moves, for always knowing where and when to put themselves in the best position to succeed.

I tried to use what they did as a blueprint.

Another guy I admired was Tom Waddle, who played for the Bears from 1989 to 1994. I had sort of adopted him as one of my all-time favorites because I identified with his style and with his career. He, too, was an underdog, getting cut several times before he finally made it. The guy never wore gloves; he just wore tape around his fingers. And he was always covered with grass stains and clumps of sod from diving all over the place to catch the ball.

This was my idea of someone who played the game the way it was meant to be played.

When I showed up two days later for our next practice, I saw more evidence that I might be sticking around. There was a nameplate over my locker that said 80 CHREBET. Then, when I walked into the receivers' meeting, I noticed there were only three other guys there besides me: Yarborough, Davis, and a new guy, Charles Wilson, a six-year veteran who had been picked up the day before in a trade with Tampa Bay. Allen and Ceaser were among the players waived in the final cut to fifty-three.

But I still wasn't sure where I stood. Did I actually make the team or was there a chance I was going to be cut after all? I knew we were getting ready for our season opener the following weekend in Miami and that I was a part of those preparations. But I didn't understand the whole process of setting a roster. I didn't know how final that final cut really was.

That didn't stop my teammates and other people from congratulating me, though. Even John Schmitt, who at the time was the lone previous Hofstra player to make an NFL roster, stopped by practice to shake my hand. John was the Jets' center from 1964 to 1973. He showed me his Super Bowl III championship ring, which was pretty impressive. I told him I hoped I could get one of my own someday.

John knew, better than anyone, just how great the distance is from our alma mater to the Jets' training complex, even though it is right on the Hofstra campus.

"I remember all the players would stand up at dinner and say who they were and where they were from. You know, 'I'm Joe Namath, quarterback, Alabama,' " Schmitt told reporters of his rookie camp in '64. "So I said, 'John Schmitt, offensive center, Hofstra University.' And everyone wanted to know if that was a girls' school."

I had promised my parents I would call them as soon as I knew anything. But as far as I was concerned, I still didn't know. Several hours went by before I finally made the call.

"Hi, Mom," I said, whispering so no one would hear me in the locker room.

"Well, what's going on?" she said.

"I don't know."

"What do you mean, 'I don't know'!"

"I saw the list of guys who have been cut, and my name wasn't on it. But I don't know if that means I've made it."

"So ask somebody!"

"I'm not asking anyone."

"Why not?"

"Because I think the less I say about it, the better off I'll be."

"There has to be some way for you to find out, something that indicates you're on the team."

"Well, there is a plate over my locker with my name and number eighty on it."

"For crying out loud, son. If they gave you a locker with your name and number on it, I think that means you've made it."

"Maybe. But I don't know."

Instead of celebrating, which a lot of my relatives and friends were doing, I pretty much kept myself in a fog of uncertainty. I refused to take anything for granted and assume my trial period was over. I kept thinking, *At some point, I'm going to get a tap on the shoulder from The Turk.* I kept envisioning Harry Fisher escorting me out of the locker room and out of the gate—and this time there would be no getting back in.

When training camp broke and we had to move out of the dorms, most of the new guys who made the team went looking for places to rent in and around Hempstead, which, even though our games are at Giants Stadium, is where we have our daily meetings and practices. All except me. I moved in with one of my former college teammates, a running back named Mark Cox who had a little basement apartment down the street from Hofstra. Mark let me sleep on his couch. We weren't in the best of neighborhoods, but we did have a cop living upstairs, so that made us feel kind of safe.

Three weeks into the regular season, Rich Kotite finally came up to me and said, "Are you really sleeping on someone's couch?"

"Yes."

"Why?"

"Because I'm not really sure what's going on yet as far as how much longer I'm going to be on the team."

Richie smiled and shook his head.

"Listen, go and get yourself a place to live. I have a feeling you're going to be around for a while."

I was thrilled to hear that and I believed he was sincere. But rather than go through the hassle of moving, I just started paying Mark three hundred dollars a month, which was still a heck of a lot cheaper than it would have been to live anywhere else around there.

The night before our first game in Miami one of our public relations people brought me into the production meeting at our hotel with the TV announcers who would do the game for NBC. The idea is for them to sit around separately with the coaches and a couple of players from each team to pick up some extra background, anecdotes, and any other tidbits of inside information that might be useful during the broadcast.

Just as we were getting ready to leave, Cris Collinsworth, the former Cincinnati receiver who was the color analyst for the game, said, "Good luck out there."

"Thanks," I said, shaking his hand.

Then Cris decided to share something with me that I guess was meant to be a motivational boost, although it seemed much more like an effort to make sure I wouldn't sleep that night.

"You know, I dropped the first pass that was ever thrown to me," he said. "So don't feel nervous out there."

I'm thinking, *Why is he telling me this? Is it something he likes to share with all rookie receivers he talks to the night before their first game? Is it one of those misery-loves-company deals where if I drop the first pass that comes to me, he won't feel so bad about his drop?*

Anyway, when we got to Joe Robbie Stadium (which was what the place was called at the time before it became Pro Player Stadium) on September 3, 1995, there was, indeed, one player on our team who was just bursting with anxiety. He was jumping around like a maniac. He was ready to go, ready to get his NFL career under way.

No, I'm not talking about myself.

I'm talking about tight end Kyle Brady, who is now a member of the Jacksonville Jaguars. As I would find out through four years of being his teammate and roommate on the road, it was not unusual for Kyle to get pretty worked up before a game. But he was especially pumped to face the Dolphins because there was so much at stake for him. He was the number-one pick that a lot of Jet fans wished had been a player at another position, such as defensive tackle. He had a big contract. And if Kyle didn't perform great right off the bat, he knew that he and the team were going to hear about it.

Me? I can honestly say that, despite Collinsworth's little "pep talk," I was as relaxed as could be. I had my family in the stands, along with my high school football coach, Huff, whom I had promised to take to that first game if I made the team. I was smiling, laughing, having a great time. My attitude was: *Hey, I'm not even supposed to be here. No one is expecting much out of me. So, as long as I don't screw up too bad, anything I do is going to be positive.*

When we took the field for pregame warm-ups, I started thinking about that first official pass that would come my way. And I was saying to myself, *Let me just get a nice little crossing pattern, maybe a hitch. Just something five or ten yards, something easy to get that first one under my belt.*

Apparently, though, I forgot to convey those wishes to Boomer Esiason.

Halfway through the second quarter, while still awaiting

that first chance to catch the ball, I ran a corner route. Boomer just threw one out there with a lot of steam on it. My first thought was: *I'm never going to catch up to this damn thing.* Then I just kind of laid out as it sailed over my shoulder, stretched my arms as far as they would go, and caught the very back tip of the ball. I mean, my fingernails turned white as I squeezed as hard as I could, trying to hold on. I was able to tuck the ball in as I rolled to the ground for a twenty-seven yard gain to the Miami forty-eight.

I still consider that first catch as probably my best in the pros.

I wound up grabbing two more balls, which gave me three on the day for forty-three yards. That was the good news.

The bad news was that the Dolphins pounded us, 52–14. Whatever joy I felt over having a successful NFL debut was buried by the embarrassment of the final score.

What a way to start a season.

Because Charles Wilson scored our only offensive touchdown on a nice catch against Miami, he earned a starting spot for our second game, against the Indianapolis Colts in Giants Stadium. And the man he replaced was not me, but Yarborough.

After beginning training camp at the bottom of a ten-man depth chart, I was suddenly the number-one receiver for the Jets.

Do I believe in miracles? Yes.

My belief became even stronger when I reached the second major milestone of my career that day by catching my first

NFL touchdown. It came on a five-yard pass from Boomer to put us in front of the Colts, 24–3, early in the third quarter.

I would love to tell you what a joyful, magical experience it was and describe every second of it in detail. But I won't. Actually, I can't because what happened later in the game pretty much erased whatever memory I have of the play, including the joy and the magic.

The first thing that went wrong was our falling asleep and allowing the Colts to score the next twenty-four points to tie the game and force overtime. We won the coin toss, took the kickoff, and quickly faced third-and-ten from our twenty. I went streaking down the left sideline and Boomer threw me a bomb that kind of hung up a little bit but that I was all ready to catch. A defender jumped in front of me to try to knock the ball down, but he never touched it. I was at the Colts' forty, waiting for the tip.

Instead, the ball came straight to me . . . and I let it sail right through my arms.

If I had caught it, we would have almost been in field goal range for Nick Lowery, who just happened to be the most accurate kicker in NFL history. But because I didn't, we had to punt. Barely three minutes later, Mike Cofer kicked a fifty-two-yard field goal. Final score: Colts 27, Jets 24.

Afterward, while fighting back tears, I told reporters that I accepted full responsibility for the loss.

"I cost my team a big play," I said. "If I catch it, I'm a hero. If I drop it, I'm a goat. The papers will say I'm a goat, and I am. Before that, I had the best moments of my life.

"That was the worst."

In the blink of an eye, I went from being unbelievably happy about getting in the end zone for that very first time as a pro and feeling just a little more comfortable with what I was doing for a living to waking up the next day and having my family and my friends and myself read and hear and see that I had choked.

It was a defining moment in my career because until then, all I had seen in the papers were hometown-boy-makes-good stories: CHREBET GETS CONTRACT! . . . CHREBET MAKES TEAM! . . . CHREBET WINS STARTING JOB!" Now, all of a sudden, I was getting my first taste of bad publicity. Now, all of a sudden, it was: "Oh, yeah, we knew all along he couldn't cut it in the NFL."

It wasn't anything vicious. And it wasn't anything that I didn't anticipate. It was just amazing how fast it went from people expecting nothing from me to accepting nothing short of greatness. Maybe I was starting to think that way a little bit myself, because when I did screw up, no one was harder on me than I was.

Everything had been going along so smoothly that I didn't prepare myself for any sort of fall.

I guess a lot of people were looking to see how I would handle what had happened against the Colts when we played our third game, which was also at home, against Jacksonville.

I gave them my answer at the end of our first drive. That was when I caught an eleven-yard touchdown pass from Boomer.

The throw was actually intended for Wilson, who was running toward the corner of the end zone while I was just running a clearing route. But as Wilson was being hit, the ball bounced off his hands and I grabbed it out of the air for my second NFL score. My rule has always been: Anything that's close to me, I'm going to go for it because you never know when or if you'll ever get another one.

I finished with seven catches for fifty-eight yards as we finally got our first win of the season, 27–10. Maybe that showed everyone how I was going to stand up to the pressure of having my first bad game.

Of course, as the year went on, it became clear that no one on the team, myself included, played as well as we needed to play.

Probably the lowest of our many low points that season was a 47–10 home loss to Oakland. The coaches had wanted rookie Carl Greenwood to start at cornerback, but he couldn't because of dehydration he had suffered in the middle of the week, apparently because he skipped too many meals. So another rookie, Vance Joseph, who had been a backup quarterback and running back at Colorado, played corner for the first time in his life that day. And the receiver he had to cover was none other than Tim Brown, whom Vance gave plenty of room to catch a bunch of passes, two for touchdowns.

The following week we traveled to Buffalo. Everett McIver, a converted defensive lineman, was going to play his first game at offensive tackle against Bruce Smith, only one of the greatest pass rushers in NFL history. Poor Boomer.

In the second quarter, Everett had a false start, but the officials took their time blowing a whistle. So Bruce came around him like an out-of-control freight train and blasted Boomer, knocking him unconscious for a good two minutes. It was one of the hardest hits I've ever seen another player take. Boomer wouldn't return until late in the season. We lost that game by nineteen points.

It had been a tradition for Mr. Leon Hess, the late owner of the Jets, to give the players a pep talk during our Thanksgiving Day practice. We had a 2–9 record at that point, and there were still five games left. If there was any year we needed words of encouragement, that was it. And that was exactly what he gave us, pointing out that we hadn't quit in our previous game, a 28–26 loss to the Bills.

"You came back and learned you can do a hell of a job," Mr. Hess said. "Let's go out with dignity—and show them we're not a bunch of horses' asses."

I always had the greatest amount of respect for Mr. Hess, as did everyone else in the NFL and the entire sports world. His death in May of 1999 brought sadness to all of us in the Jets' family. I will always remember him for his quiet, classy manner. But he also knew when to step forward and make himself heard. And because he didn't do it that often, it usually had a lot of impact.

Mr. Hess's words on that Thanksgiving Day practice certainly had an impact, because three days later we beat the Seahawks in Seattle.

Unfortunately, that would be our last win of the season. We ended up with a 3–13 record, worst in the league.

I wanted to feel good about getting the contract, making the team, winning a starting spot, and being one of only two players on offense to start all sixteen games (guard Roger Duffy was the other).

I wanted to feel good about finishing the year with sixty-six catches, most ever by a Jets' rookie and the second-highest rookie total in the NFL that year behind the sixty-seven of Seattle first-rounder Joey Galloway from Ohio State. I wanted to feel good about having seven hundred and twenty-six yards receiving, second-highest rookie total in Jets' history behind the seven hundred and forty Wesley Walker had in 1977, and four touchdowns.

I couldn't.

I was never just happy to be there. I was never just giddy about thinking, *Hey, I'm an NFL player. Look at me.* My thinking had always been: *I made this team. Now I'm going to do something with it.* I was over the excitement of wearing the "NFL player" label long before that first game in Miami.

Once I saw how the season was going, how the losses were mounting, my only thought was, *I hope this is not going to be like this forever.* I didn't know what the expectations were for us before the season, and I didn't care. I just know that thirteen losses were not what I expected.

And along with a record like that comes a whole lot of grief from every direction. You and your teammates and coaches get a steady pounding from fans, from the radio, from TV, from the papers. It was the first time I had ever seen anyone attack my manhood, which was exactly what was happening to all of us because what was being criticized was what we did for a living. When a reporter or a lawyer or an accountant does something wrong, a certain number of people might know about it.

But when we do something wrong, millions of people know about it and they make damn sure we hear about it. There were almost sixty-nine thousand people at the Raiders' game, our biggest crowd of the season. By the end of the third quarter, with Oakland holding a thirty-point lead, the crowd began chanting, "Let's go, Raiders!"

For me, that type of fan reaction was a much tougher adjustment than going from catching passes in Division 1-AA to catching them in the NFL.

Late in my rookie season, I was barely able to lift my right arm because of the shoulder injury I had suffered in training camp. I wasn't able to hide it any longer. I took some cortisone shots and tried to manage as best as possible. But late in the season, it got so bad that I could hardly lift my right arm, which obviously became a problem when I had to go for those high passes.

So at the end of the year, Richie came up to me and said, "I know your shoulder's been bothering you. You've got to have surgery on it."

I knew he was right. My shoulder felt like I had ten pounds of crap stuffed into a five-pound bag. It became so tight that it was practically dead. But I still didn't want the surgery. I worried that any sort of operation might set me back as far as offseason conditioning and hurt my chances of being able to make the team the following year. Besides, I had gone through a whole season that way; I just figured I could keep fighting through it.

That isn't the way things are done in the NFL, however. If you have a body part that isn't working right, it gets fixed or you don't play.

"I'm not asking you to do this," Richie said. "I'm telling you that you don't have a choice. You have to get this done. Now!"

Three days before Amy and I were heading to the Poconos for our annual Valentine's Day getaway, I had arthroscopic surgery on my right shoulder. What a perfect way to get yourself ready for a weekend of skiing and snowmobiling.

My labrum, which keeps the rotator cuff in place, was detached, so the doctor had to tack it back down. I also had some bone spurs that needed to be shaved. It was the best move I could have made because my shoulder was trouble-free after that.

The only thing more incredible than getting a six-figure salary to play football—something that I would gladly do for free—is getting paid extra just for working out in the offseason. When that happened in my first offseason with the Jets, I thought it was hysterical. It's basically a bribe for coming in to try and help yourself, which, in turn, is going to help the team.

Another thing that took some getting used to was having

people treat me differently after I went from blending into the crowd like any other twenty-two-year-old kid from North Jersey to being recognized almost everywhere you go.

When you're in college and you couldn't afford stuff, you still had to pay for things, like a meal at a restaurant. Now, when you have all of this money and you can afford a lot more, you hear, "No, no, it's on the house . . . it's on me."

It's nice to know that people think I'm doing something special. I like it, I accept it, but I don't take advantage of it. I've never been one to say, "Listen, I play football. Take care of me." I'll just say, "Reservation for Wayne Chrebet," and sometimes it will go from an hour and a half wait to "Be right with you . . . and here's complimentary bottle of wine."

I'm still a lot more comfortable eating a Whopper in the parking lot of Burger King at two in the morning than I am going to some fancy restaurant. In fact, that's how Amy and I spent our first date.

And I still love to go to places like Rose's Pizzeria in Garfield. It's the best pizza in town. I've been there a thousand times for my usual order—a couple of slices of Sicilian, with nothing on them except sauce and cheese. I will forever be associated with Rose's. And the owners know that they don't have to put up a sign that says THIS IS WHERE WAYNE CHREBET GETS HIS PIZZA to keep me coming back. About the only thing that's changed from when I first started going to the place as a kid is that they now have my picture up on the wall . . . right next to Don Corleone.

I'm appreciative of the opportunities that come with being a professional athlete—being able to go places that I would probably never be able to go as a nonplayer, meeting actors and sports figures that I would probably never be able to meet otherwise. I've made some great friends that way, such as Jayson Williams, All-Star center for the New Jersey Nets, and Jason Sehorn and Michael Strahan of the Giants. In the offseason, I can always count on Strahan to show me exactly how bad my golf game is compared to his.

Sometimes I'll get to show off my basketball skills in a little one-on-one with Jayson Williams. You don't know what it's like to be on the receiving end of an in-your-face jam until you've had it done to you by a six-foot-ten NBA player.

As enjoyable and entertaining as my off-field life can be, I just don't see any reason to take advantage of who I am or what I do. I'm still amazed when I go to an appearance and someone will come up to me and say, "It's great to see how normal you are."

I stop and think, *Normal? It's actually a compliment when someone calls you normal?*

But the fact is, when some pro athletes deal with the public, they think that they're owed something. I've just never been able to relate to that. I'm not curing cancer. I play football; I'm an entertainer. People appreciate what I do and maybe they think I'm personable, but I'm not doing anything that the world can't do without.

I mean, football is a great sport. I think it's one of the greatest sports ever. It's entertaining and I'm glad to be a part of it, especially the tradition of it. But it is not a life-and-death thing. And I don't know why there are people who do what I do who can't seem to understand that—who think the public should feel indebted to them for offering the services of catching a football. I'm not mentioning names and I'm not saying everyone is like that.

I just know that isn't how my parents raised me and it isn't the type of behavior they would ever condone, no matter how old I am. If I have to wait for a table at a restaurant, I'll wait. If I have to pay a cover charge to get into a nightclub, I'll pay a cover charge.

I'm not going to get into a fight and end up on "Sports-Center" in handcuffs.

Another funny thing about the success I had once I was on the team: Sports agents who didn't want to know my name when I was in college started falling all over each other to get me to leave Art Weiss, so they could take me on as a client. They promised they would be able to get me a big contract, really set me up well, but I turned them all down. I wanted to stick with Art, the guy who believed in me when no one else was giving me the time of day and someone that I was very comfortable with.

I remember one agent who constantly called me for us to get together. Finally I agreed to go to dinner with him at this nice steakhouse on Long Island, just to get him off my back. He was a younger guy, about my size and physically fit. We took my car.

The thing I didn't like about him right off the bat was that he was a nonstop talking machine, telling me all the great things he was going to do for me. I hate it when people just talk and talk and talk to hear themselves speak.

He started showing me paperwork about what kind of deal he thought he could get me and so forth. Then, after a long dinner, we headed back for his car. As we drove, he asked me what kind of person I wanted in there negotiating for me.

I decided it was time to have a little fun.

"Basically, I want someone like myself, but with the knowledge of contracts," I said. "I want a real bulldog in there."

"I'm your guy, I'm your guy," he said.

"I want someone who doesn't back down to anything, who can't be rattled. He's going to make my case without pushing the wrong buttons, you know?"

"Oh, yeah, yeah. I can do that for you. I'm telling you, man, I'm your guy, I'm your guy."

We pulled into the lot where his car was parked. I lowered the radio and, with the most serious look I could muster, I said, "OK, listen, this is what we're going to do. We're going to get out of this car and we're going to fight. And if you win, you can represent me. And if I beat you up . . . I beat you up."

He was shocked, of course. At first, he could barely answer me.

Then finally he said, "Fight? Are you serious?"

"Yes," I said, trying hard not to laugh while maintaining a stern look.

"Well . . . uh . . . I guess . . . uh."

"Man, forget it. Good to meet you. Take care."

This guy spent a whole night telling me what a tough, relentless negotiator he was, and I had just rattled him without any problem. If I could make him break like that, what was Bill Parcells going to do to him?

When you have a 3–13 record, the offseason is going to bring a lot of changes. Ours certainly did.

We picked up all kinds of new faces in an effort to help improve our passing game. Neil O'Donnell, who was fresh off of leading Pittsburgh to the Super Bowl, was signed to replace Boomer, who signed with Arizona two months later. Frank Reich was acquired from Carolina to replace Bubby Brister as the other backup quarterback with Glenn Foley.

We also loaded up with a lot of new receivers. We signed Jeff Graham and Webster Slaughter in free agency. We used the top overall pick of the draft on Keyshawn Johnson from USC, and our second-round choice on Alex Van Dyke from Nevada. Keyshawn and Jeff would be the new starters. I was demoted to number three.

Those moves made it pretty clear that my accomplishments as a rookie, while good enough to force some updating of the Jets' record book, did not make me any taller or Hofstra any larger than they were the previous year. I still wasn't receiving the respect I felt I was beginning to deserve.

But rather than pout or complain, I kept my mouth shut

and did whatever I was asked to do. As long as I was still on the team, I knew I could do something to make a contribution, even if it meant returning punts, which would become one of my new duties that second year.

Some things didn't change, though.

In the summer before training camp, I played in a celebrity golf tournament. A bunch of us were assigned to play in groups with corporate types. So when I got together with my group, one of my playing partners looked at me and said, "Are you our caddie?"

"No," I said, trying to smile while squeezing the shaft of my nine-iron almost hard enough to leave dents in it. "I'm playing with you guys."

Seeing a perfect opportunity to bust some chops, I never told him my name and just got in the passenger side of his golf cart, propping my feet up on the dashboard. A short while later, another golfer walking by recognized me and said, "Hey, there's Wayne Chrebet!"

I started smiling. And the guy who thought I was a caddie said, "Oh, I'm so sorry. I didn't know it was you."

"Don't worry about it. I get that all the time."

I would still get a lot of playing time as the number-three receiver, especially on third down. I have always felt that third down is my down. That's when I want the ball the most. I pride myself on living in the middle of the field, where a lot of receivers won't go. And our new offensive coordinator, Ron

Erhardt, who was hired from the Steelers, was determined to put me there as often as possible.

I actually saw some advantages to my new role. I was happy to let defenses concentrate on the other receivers outside and forget about me in the slot. That gave me the chance to sit in those open areas all day and catch a ton of balls.

Adjusting to a new quarterback wasn't hard at all. I had very good chemistry with Neil because I worked out with him a couple of times a week in the offseason, as I did with Foley.

I got a chance to play with Frank for a while because Neil wound up missing ten games with two different injuries. Six games into the season, he tore up his shoulder. Then, during warm-ups before his return game, he did the freakiest thing of all by tearing a calf muscle while just backpedaling.

That was typical of the kind of season we were having.

Frank and I also developed good chemistry right away. The amazing thing about his ball was that he would throw it hard but it hit your hands soft. Frank was a lot like Boomer— just a smart guy who knew football, loved football, played hard, and never wanted to pat himself on the back.

Like so many other fans, I will never forget Frank's miracle game for the Buffalo Bills when he led them from thirty-two points behind to beat the Houston Oilers in overtime in a wild-card playoff game after the 1992 season. I was in my second year at Hofstra at the time, and I was going to a movie with my parents. We were listening to the game on the car radio and, because we were running late, my parents wanted to get inside the theater as fast as possible. I told them I would wait in the car because the Bills were coming back and I just had to know how that game ended.

Afterward, I walked into the theater and told my father, "They came back and beat the Oilers."

"You've got to be kidding me," he said.

"Nope. Frank brought them back."

Frank also led the greatest comeback in college football when his University of Maryland team battled back from a thirty-one-point deficit to beat the University of Miami.

But he never said too much about either of those history-making games because he just wasn't the type of guy who would talk about himself. He was a classy individual and someone I still consider a good friend.

I thought we had hit rock-bottom at 3–13.

Going through a 1–15 season, as we did in 1996, was a nightmare to end all nightmares.

I know every player and coach on a team with a horrible record says this, but it's true: We weren't *that* bad. Honest!

We had something like six games where we were winning at halftime, then we blew each one in the second half. We would lose by one point . . . or by three points . . . or by a touchdown. We were just good enough to compete with most of the teams we played—and just bad enough to find a way to lose. The lone exception was our ten-point win against Boomer's Arizona Cardinals.

Probably our weirdest game of that season was our 21–7

home loss to Indianapolis in Week Two. History was made when play was held up for thirty-two minutes because of lightening.

If anything bizarre was going to happen to us, it was going to happen that year.

Another game that will always stick with me was our Week Seven trip to Jacksonville. With Keyshawn and Jeff hurt, Alex, my good friend and roommate on the road, and I became the starters. Frank was starting in place of Neil. And once the game got going, it felt like Hofstra at Delaware all over again. Everything Frank threw, I caught. It didn't matter what patterns I was running or what coverages the Jaguars were playing, I found openings all over the place—and Frank kept getting me the ball.

When the day was over, I had career highs with twelve receptions for a hundred and sixty-two yards, including a twelve-yard touchdown. Eight of my catches went for first downs. And Jacksonville, in only its second year of existence, was doing everything it could to self-destruct, with fifteen penalties for a hundred and twenty-three yards.

Yet, in the end, the only numbers that really mattered were Jaguars 21, Jets 17. All because we couldn't hold on to a 14–3 lead in the second quarter.

I got the living hell beat out of me that day. I had welts and bruises everywhere. I was bleeding long after we left the field. And I didn't care. When you're pouring everything you have into a game, throwing your body all over the field, it can be contagious. It can turn a game around, maybe even a whole season. I have always believed that willpower can be a very powerful thing, and I was trying, along with Frank and others, to will us a victory that day.

But when it was over, nothing was more painful to me than the fact we would be flying home with another loss stuck in our throats and an 0–7 record.

The following week we lost yet another heartbreaker, 25–22, to the Bills. I thought we were going to come out on top that day after Frank threw one of the greatest passes I have ever seen, threading the ball through double coverage on third down to hit me for a twenty-one-yard touchdown to tie the game at 22–22 with just under two minutes left in the fourth quarter. I just closed my eyes, caught the ball, and went sliding on my back in the end zone.

I closed my eyes again a short while later when Steve Christie kicked a field goal with ten seconds left to make 0-for-the-first-half-of-the-season. Counting the last four games of '95, we were 0–12.

And things were only going to get worse!

During the season like we had in '96, you tend to stay home a little bit more than usual because you just don't want to hear all of the crap being dished out. I can't say that I had any real problems out in public, but after a while, it got a little tiring when people would come up to you and say things like, "Come on, you guys. Don't you want to win?"

Of course we wanted to win. No one wanted to win more

or was hurt more by the losing than we were. It killed me everytime I walked off that field, knowing we had let another one get away.

I had to laugh when someone would come up to me and say, "Please, win just this one time—for me."

I'd be thinking, *All right, just because you said that, we are going to win now. We didn't have a reason to win before. Now we've got one. And we're going to win our next game, just for you, buddy. Now what's your name, so I can mention it on the radio after the game?*

I have always gotten a lot of fan mail, which I greatly appreciate. But that year, a lot of the letters included suggestions for Richie to help get us back on track. You'd see things like: "Maybe you should tell him to trade for . . ." or "Maybe you should tell him to start running this play . . ."

I think some of those people had a little bit too much time on their hands, but I understood their frustration. I was a fan long before I was a player. I yelled and screamed and was ready to tear my hair out all of those times my Giants would lose a close one.

I'm still a fan. I still root with all my heart for the Yankees and I still consider the Giants "my Giants" because that's what they have always been to me and the rest of my family.

But when you're doing this stuff for a living, your outlook changes. It's impossible not to take the awful things being said about you and your team personally. So I did my best to avoid reading the papers and listening to the radio and watching TV.

On the other hand, my father read, heard, and saw everything. And I do mean everything, searching for even the smallest reference—good or bad—to his baby boy. As far as I'm concerned, any criticism directed toward the team is directed toward me because I'm part of the team.

But for the most part, there weren't too many negative things said specifically about me in 1996 because I think there were some people out there who at least appreciated the fact that you were still trying, no matter how long the losing streak got.

Even though I made only nine starts—including the last three games, while Jeff was out with turf toe—I wound up leading the team with eighty-four catches for nine hundred and nine yards and three touchdowns. My two-year total of a hundred and fifty receptions is still the most any receiver in NFL history has had in his first two seasons.

I also returned twenty-eight punts that year for a hundred and thirty-nine yards, but that was one job I truly hated. All you were really doing most of the time was making sure you fielded the ball—which I could do with no problem—but then you'd get killed from ten different directions.

I was glad that would be my one and only season as a punt returner.

As usual, I had my family's support to help me get through all of the hurt and disappointment that came from the mounting losses and dwindling crowds in Giants Stadium. Just like every year that I've been in the pros, my parents were there for me every Sunday—home or away—with Dad wearing a Jets jersey with my number. Jen joined them on a lot of road trips, too, and all three of them still insist on paying their own way.

I'll admit, it was a little awkward at first, a grown man having his parents come to all of his games. That obviously wasn't the case with every player on the team or even most of them. But after a while I finally understood I must be the luckiest person in the world to still have a family that's that interested in what I do.

Our family is also blessed to have tons of terrific friends who faithfully show up for every home game, win or lose. In '96, one of the greatest things—and, at that point, the only thing—for me to look forward to after a home game was the mammoth tailgate party that a bunch of friends of the family began putting together in my rookie year and have kept going strong ever since.

You can't believe the magnitude of what goes on in parking lot 8B. It looks like a carnival. There are tents, TEAM 80 and JETS banners all over the place, a specially made street sign that says WAYNE CHREBET BLVD., strung-up lights, microwaves, portable generators, and food like you have never seen—all prepared and provided by family friends whose love and devotion is amazing. Sometimes they will do themes, like Italian Day. And almost as unbelievable as what they do before a game is that, after packing it all up just before kickoff, they pull it all back out after the game.

I used to stop by the postgame tailgate party, but unfortunately, it's almost impossible now because of all of the people coming by for autographs. There's just no way you can visit with your family or friends and get a bite of that delicious food without autograph seekers thinking that you're being rude by ignoring them, and I don't want that to happen. So usually after a game, I will get together with my family and Amy at a restaurant.

During that disastrous '96 season, Dad always did his best to try to keep my spirits up. But it reached a point where little he or anyone else could say could make me feel better about what was going on. After one of our losses, he came up to me and said, "Well, at least you did good, Butch."

And I said, "But we lost. If I had a good game, it doesn't matter. You show that you're doing your job, fine. And maybe you'll have a job the following season. But when you lose, everybody's blamed."

When you're a head coach with a 4–28 record in two seasons, blame falls on your head like a pile of bricks.

Sadly, that was the case with Rich Kotite, who would be out as coach right after the 1996 season.

I never thought he deserved all of the blame for those two horrible years, but he accepted all of it, which I liked and respected. Richie never tried to push it onto the players and say it was our fault. It wasn't like: "Hey, if we win it is because of me, and if we lose it is because of them."

The fact is, he coached some unbelievable teams in Philadelphia before he came to the Jets. He is a good coach. He definitely knows his stuff, especially when it comes to offense.

Richie believed in giving players a lot of freedom and I think, in the end, that was what hurt him the most because a lot of players we had took advantage of that. He didn't have the Reggie Whites or the Seth Joyners or Jerome Browns, guys that he had with the Eagles who could run the team and keep everyone in line for him. He didn't try to kill us in training camp. He liked to say, "Just do your thing," but the kind of team we had didn't respond to that.

I know I loved being around the guy, even when he was puffing on one of those stinky cigars before practice. He cracked me up with the things he said in his deep voice and in that thick Brooklyn accent. Anytime you did something good on the field, no matter what, he would say, "That away, babe!"

Everyone on the team was "babe" to him.

He was left-handed, and when he spoke, he would always have that left hand moving. He was a really good boxer in his college days. Before transferring to Wagner, a small college on Staten Island, Richie was heavyweight champion at the University of Miami as a freshman. He even sparred with Muhammad Ali at Angelo Dundee's Fifth Street Gym in Miami.

Richie liked to give you the kind of advice that you'd expect from an ex-fighter: "When you're walking down the street and you see three guys coming at you, you pick the biggest one and you smack him right in the mouth."

Whatever you say, Rich. Just make sure you're around to bail me out of jail and to pay for the lawsuit.

I am forever indebted to him just for seeing something in me that maybe no one else saw—enough to just give me a chance. I obviously showed him, as well as everyone else, that I could play in the NFL. But he didn't have to let me start in that final preseason game against Cincinnati in 1995 or, for that matter, give me the opportunity to come to camp in the first place.

Maybe he did it because he, too, had gone from a small college to the NFL, playing tight end and special teams for the Giants and Steelers, and he could relate with what I was going through.

Maybe he did it in passing. Maybe he did it as a joke. Maybe he did it by accident.

It doesn't matter why. Because once I showed what I could do, Richie let me run with it. He wanted to see how far I could go.

People say that the best thing Richie ever did when he was with the Jets was give me my big break. I'm sure, at the start, he caught some flak for that. And I'm glad that I showed all of the doubters that Richie knew what he was doing by letting me play and start that first season. I realized what the ramifications would have been if I didn't perform well.

In a big way, he put himself on the line for me.

Our last game of the 1996 season was at home against Miami. Two days earlier, Rich announced that he was stepping aside as coach after that game.

After I caught a nine-yard touchdown pass to pull us within three points late in the game, I ran over to give him the ball. I wish we could have given him a victory, too, but we lost, 31–28. The game ended on a fumble by me after I caught a fourteen-yard pass. Maybe I was pressing too hard.

I don't care how much people badmouth Richie or his Jets' record, I will never be one of them. I am always going to stick up for the guy.

I am faithful to people who have faith in me.

12

Rescued by a Tuna

I had always heard the horror stories about Bill Parcells—how he didn't get along with a lot of the people who played for him or worked with him, how he was a master of intimidation, how he could just carve you up with one slash of his tongue, such as when he called Terry Glenn, his top receiver in New England, "She."

I also understood that Bill was the kind of guy that if you played for him the way he expected you to play, he would still

be on your back, but not nearly as much as if you were just going through the motions and collecting a paycheck. If you
really played for the man, if you played with all of your heart
and soul, you would not have a problem.

When I saw that Bill was going to replace Rich Kotite in
1997, I thought, *This is the kind of coach that I want.*

It wasn't that I needed him or anyone else to tell me to
play with desire and passion. I had been doing that my whole
life. It was just that when the man known as "the Big Tuna"
arrived, it got everybody on the same page—at least everybody
that could handle the heavy demands that went with playing
for him. I liked that.

I was looking forward to his military, it's-my-way-or-the-
highway style. No matter how hard you're already playing, it
makes you play harder. I was also looking forward to being
coached by someone I had the utmost respect for—someone I
had idolized growing up as a fan of the Giants, whom he had
coached from 1983 to 1990.

I wasn't there to lose. I mean, I was being paid good
money, living the greatest life I could have ever imagined. But
it was horrible to experience all of that losing in your first two
seasons of pro ball. It just left you constantly frustrated and
humiliated and depressed. We needed some direction. We
needed some hope.

Once Bill took over my first thought was: *This is going to be
turned right around pretty quickly.*

Everyone knew that he was going to make changes. You
don't inherit a team that has lost twenty-eight of its last
thirty-two games without a major overhaul. And we were

Celebrating my first contract with the Jets with my agent and close friend, Art Weiss, who believed in me when so many others didn't. *(Brian M. Ballweg)*

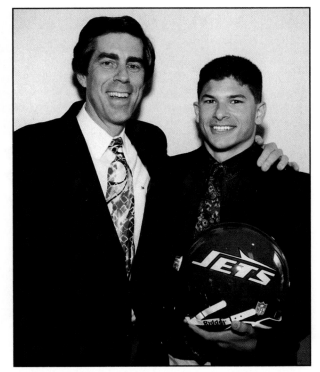

In the middle of the crowd before my first preseason game on August 5, 1995, in Tampa. *(Author's collection)*

Concentrating on the action while catching my breath.
(Richard A. Brightly)

Pulling away from a tackler. *(Richard A. Brightly)*

Hanging out with a bunch of my friends while shooting a United Way commercial. *(Art Weiss)*

While in San Francisco for our '98 season opener, I got together with fellow Hofstra alums Niners defensive back Lance Schulters and offensive tackle Dave Fiore. *(Al Pereira/New York Jets)*

Bill Parcells always has his game face on. *(Richard A. Brightly)*

Joe Namath, the greatest Jet of them all, was nice enough to pose for this picture with our family. *(Author's collection)*

With Dad, my best friend and number-one fan. *(Author's collection)*

Going in motion. *(Richard A. Brightly)*

Bobby Hamilton and I couldn't wait to give Bill Parcells a Gatorade shower after we clinched the 1998 AFC East championship in Buffalo. (©1998 Joe Traver/Reuters)

Portrait of a happy family. (*Author's collection*)

Dad, Mom, and Jen were there when I received the Unsung Hero Award from the NFL Players Association. (*Author's collection*)

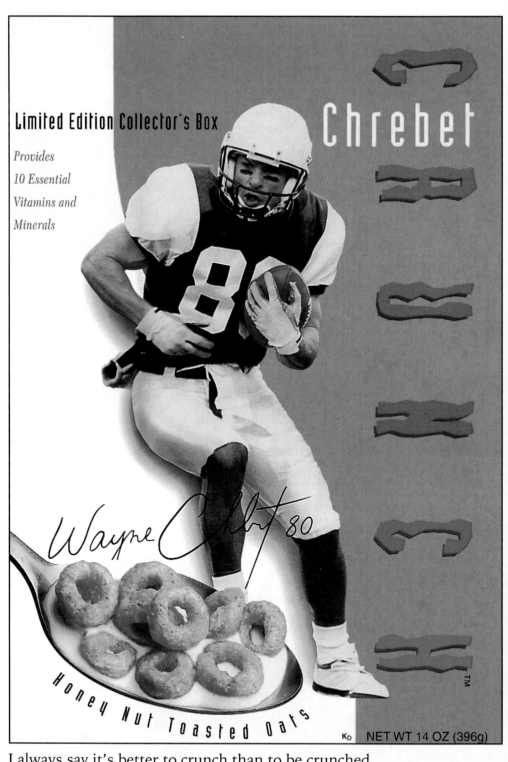

Limited Edition Collector's Box

Provides
10 Essential
Vitamins and
Minerals

Chrebet

CRUNCH™

Wayne Chrebet 80

Honey Nut Toasted Oats

NET WT 14 OZ (396g)

I always say it's better to crunch than to be crunched.
(PLB Sports, Inc., Pittsburgh, Pa.)

all well aware of Bill's habit of bringing in *his* guys—
"Parcells's Guys"—from previous coaching stops. When he
got to New England, where he had spent the last four seasons
before coming to the Jets, he brought in players from the Giants. Now he was going to bring former Patriots and Giants to
the Jets.

"Parcells's Guys" who came aboard in '97 were linebacker Pepper Johnson, a former Giant who had been with De-
troit, and cornerback Otis Smith and safety Jerome
Henderson, both from the Patriots. Offensive tackle Jumbo Elliott, a former Giant who had played for Bill from 1988 to
1990, joined us in '96.

Being a "Parcells's Guy" means you're a winner. It also
means you probably have some years on you. But if Bill has
won with you in the past, he knows he can win with you in the
future. He knows that you know what it takes to win. He
knows that you're going to go the extra mile. He knows that
you're not going to be a cancer in the locker room. He knows
that you're going to help out the younger guys.

And if he needs someone to make an example of, he
knows that you'll take on that role, too. Even Pepper, who is
like a son to Bill, having played for him since 1986, became a
target of Tuna's wrath with the understanding that it could
help the whole team. Not that Bill said anything demeaning;
he just made certain to say it loud enough so that he could get
his point across to the rest of the players.

When they witness something like that, you know
they're thinking, *Geez, if he's yelling that loud at Pepper, we'd better get our act straight—and fast.*

Pepper not only brought a lot of experience, but he did a hell of a job playing defense for us. Anything you could ask for in a game, Pepper was there to deliver—and he'd knock the crap out of anyone who crossed his path. If you're lined up across from a linebacker who hits like that, you're going to think twice about coming through the middle with your head down.

Pepper did a great job of keeping our defense together— verbally, as well as with his actions. When things are going bad in a game, it's so easy to reach a stage where everyone starts pointing fingers and the unit begins to unravel. A veteran like Pepper can sense when that sort of thing is coming, and he knows just what to say to make it go away.

There are always points like that during the course of a year. Even if you go 16–0, there will come a time in a game, maybe two or three times, when you're going to start looking around and wondering, *Why did that guy miss the tackle? Why did that guy blow the coverage? Why did that guy miss the block? Why did that guy drop the ball?* Those are the kind of questions that can destroy team unity and kill your season.

The teams that stick together are the teams that win championships.

The influx of "Parcells's Guys" was obviously going to cause some "Kotite's Guys" to be pushed out, but I wasn't worried that I would be one of them. I felt that I had performed well enough overall—and especially in the four games I had played against Parcells's Patriots—to earn his respect. I figured Bill could see that I could play and that he already knew I had the kind of attitude he wanted on his team. Before our first game against New England in '96, he had some really nice things to say about me in the Boston media, which I appreciated.

Of course, I should point out that before he ever got to see me in action with the Jets, Bill, as coach of the Patriots, had joined that endless list of people who had sent rejection letters after my agent and my father sent him one of my college highlight videos. I think my dad tried not to let me see that letter because he thought it might bother me more than the others, since it came from the man whom I considered the greatest coach of them all. Maybe he thought if I read a letter from Parcells himself, saying that I wasn't worth even a look, I might get so discouraged that I would give up the whole idea of trying to play in the NFL.

But that rejection didn't bother me any more than the rest. It just gave me another person to prove wrong.

One more thing I had going for me with Parcells was the fact we are both from Bergen County. Bill, who was born in Englewood, has been calling me "homeboy" or "homey" since he coached New England. Whenever we played the Patriots, I would talk to him before the game and we would ask each other if we knew certain people from various towns. We found out that we went to a lot of the same pizza places (although Bill funded those establishments a lot better than I did). He has a house on the Jersey Shore; my family and I have been regulars at the Shore for as long as I can remember.

Parcells always likes to say to me: "Just remember that wherever you go in Bergen County, I know where you are and what you do."

Like he runs Bergen County. Like he's the number-one man there.

Come to think of it, maybe he is . . . but I'm gaining on him.

No disrespect for Richie, but the instant Bill walked into Weeb Ewbank Hall for the very first time, you could see his no-nonsense approach take hold. It was just a whole different attitude than what had been there the previous two years.

And the results showed on the field. We went 9–7 that first season and just missed the playoffs. We learned how to win again. But first, the whole team had to acquire the discipline that, for the most part, wasn't there in my first two seasons.

Bill instills that discipline by staying on top of every single thing and riding on top of every single back on his team, coaches as well as players. I don't ever remember seeing the relaxed, carefree guy that leads his players in song in that TV commercial for Tostitos chips and salsa. The Bill Parcells we see most of the time is every bit the stern, uncompromising SOB that you see in those video clips from his press conferences. Even worse. His basic approach is: "This is what we are doing and if you don't like it, leave!"

It's as simple as that.

You cannot coach or play for the man if you are thin-skinned.

I'm not saying we don't ever have fun. We do. But the only time you have fun on a Bill Parcells-coached team is when you win. Period. You could have an all-star cast of stand-up comics in that locker room. If you're on any kind of losing streak and Bill is your coach, you'll make mourners at a funeral seem hilarious.

We got off to a 1–2 start in '97, and our Monday routine during those first few weeks was to run sprints to work out the soreness and get ready for the upcoming week. Basic, boring stuff.

Then, when we went on to win our next three games, Bill started to make those Mondays more enjoyable by incorporating some little offbeat twists to the usual grind.

The best was the "The Fat Boy Relays," which we held once that first year. It worked like this: Three receivers and three defensive backs raced forty yards down and back—while each group carried the fattest offensive lineman and the fattest defensive lineman on the team. So it was me and two other receivers lugging Jumbo Elliott, all six-foot-seven and 325 pounds of him, while the DBs got to carry six-foot-three defensive tackle Ronnie Dixon, who weighs about the same. The losing team had to do extra running.

I ended up in the middle, with Jumbo's knees over my shoulders while he laid back so the other two guys could each take one of his massive arms. We were laughing so hard that we could barely stand up straight, let alone try to move. It was a struggle, but we won—and not by much.

Another time when we were on a win streak, Bill had us doing a drill where we jumped over each other. Picture a bunch of grown men playing leapfrog.

But Bill would just do little things like that to take the

edge off. He knew exactly when to ease up on the reins and let us loose a little bit.

In one of two two-game win streaks we had in '97, we took on the Minnesota Vikings at Giants Stadium. It was a game I will never forget because it was my first encounter with John Randle, the Vikings' trash-talking defensive tackle.

I usually don't like it when opponents start yapping during a game, but John's a riot. He comes up with the most outrageous things. He'll be out there barking like a dog or doing a running commentary on the entire offense, all while wearing his eyeblack like war paint.

Randle just constantly tries to get into your head and take you out of your game. Then—and this is the part I respect—he's able to back it up with his play. He is, by far, one of the best defensive linemen in the game.

I was having a pretty good day on that Sunday afternoon in 1997, running around and catching a bunch of passes. Now I'm sure some people are intimidated by Randle's antics. But almost every time I caught the ball that day, I would look at him as I walked back to our huddle.

I always like to look opponents in the eye after a catch, just to let them know that I'm not the least afraid of anything they might want to bring my way—and that I'll be back to see them again.

When I looked at Randle one time, he snarled and said, "I'm going to taste your blood, little man."

I thought it was hysterical.

John never did end up tasting my blood—or anything else inside or outside my body, for that matter. He and the rest of the Vikings just had to swallow a 23–21 loss, despite the fact we nearly blew a sixteen-point lead in the fourth quarter, which would have allowed them to tie the game and force overtime. A delay-of-game penalty by our defense gave the Vikings a chance to score a touchdown as the clock expired in regulation. But on the two-point conversion, Rick Lyle, a defensive end we had signed that year from Baltimore, snuffed out a handoff to Robert Smith, wrapping him up in the backfield before Victor Green and James Farrior came in to finish him off.

That was a statement-making win for us because it was exactly the kind of game that we would always lose the year before. It also gave us an 8–4 record, guaranteeing that we would not have a third straight year of losing.

After the season, I saw Randle at the Super Bowl in San Diego when we were both guests on a TV show called "Make Me Laugh."

"Do you remember what you said to me on the field during our game?" I said.

"I don't think so," John said. "Tell me."

"You said that you were going to taste my blood. Now what is that all about?"

"Aw, man. I'm sorry. I really am. I don't know what gets into me sometimes. I just get carried away. Sorry, man."

Here was this barking, trash-talking killer on the field,

and it turns out, once he has his war paint off and civilian clothes on, he is the biggest teddy bear you'd ever want to see.

But don't tell him *I* said that.

Bill Parcells didn't take over the Jets with any sort of patient, long-term rebuilding plan in mind. He wanted to win right away. He still does. After all, the guy doesn't want to coach forever.

So he keeps bringing in players that are going to make an immediate impact, rather than those who might be ready to help us out in a year or two or three.

In 1998, Bill gave one of the strongest indications of how fast he wanted to make us a championship contender by giving up first- and third-round draft picks to sign running back Curtis Martin as a restricted free agent from New England.

He went into the free agent market to pick up center Kevin Mawae from Seattle and another Patriot, fullback Keith Byars. He also helped the defense by getting linebacker Bryan Cox from Chicago and defensive end Anthony Pleasant from Atlanta. And late in the year he picked up Dave Meggett, an old reliable return man he had with the Giants and Patriots.

Of course, Bill's best find in free agency turned out to be a quarterback: Vinny Testaverde, who had been cut by the Baltimore Ravens.

Going into the '98 season, Bill had said to the media that Glenn Foley would be the starter, but after Vinny was brought in, it became a let's-see-what-happens kind of thing.

Just being a sports fan, I knew a lot about Vinny's background—that he had won the Heisman Trophy at Miami and that Tampa Bay had made him the top overall pick of the 1987 draft and that he signed as a free agent with the Cleveland Browns, the team that moved to Baltimore and became the Ravens.

It was said that Vinny never lived up to his lofty billing when he came out of college, but the way I saw it, he was on a franchise in Tampa Bay where he didn't have the greatest supporting cast. That became clear in 1996, when he had some good receivers with him in Baltimore—guys like Michael Jackson and Derrick Alexander. Vinny threw for more than four thousand yards and thirty-three touchdowns and went to the Pro Bowl.

People were always asking me, "What do you think of the controversy? Foley or Vinny?"

And I would always say, "It's not a problem. It's a blessing that we have two quarterbacks with that much talent, knowing that if one wasn't doing the job on a particular day, the other one could."

They both have super arms, which is a critical quality when you're competing with the bag of tricks Mother Nature likes to unleash in Giants Stadium. Until you've played on that field, you don't realize how tough it is throw a ball in those swirling winds. You look up and see which way those flags are blowing on top, you can bet the wind will be going in the opposite direction on the field. Quarterbacks that come from nice, calm, sunny weather usually struggle in our place, as evidenced by Trent Dilfer completing only two of fifteen passes for thirty-eight yards and throwing two interceptions in our 31–0 win over Tampa Bay in 1997.

It's not so easy on those of us who catch the ball, either. The quarterback can throw an out pattern three yards behind you and it ends up two yards ahead of you. If you're running a corner route and the wind's blowing left to right, you might want to leave a little extra room because that ball's going to float. But you get used to it and the longer you play there, the more you start making those adjustments without even thinking about them.

The best thing that could have ever happened to Vinny was the change of environment from Baltimore to New York, a Long Island boy coming back to his roots. The fact we had a really solid offense in place—passing and running—also gave him an opportunity to thrive.

And when it was his turn to take the reins from Glenn three weeks into the season, Vinny did a great job. He earned his second trip to the Pro Bowl and received our team's Most Valuable Player Award.

It's a tough situation for me to say that one guy is better than the other because I'm friends with both of them. And I truly didn't have a preference. I wished they could have both been in there at the same time.

Each guy brought a little something different in terms of style. Glenn's fiery. He's taking chances out there; he's running around. That's Glenn and that's how he performs well.

Vinny's a softer-spoken, conservative, consistent kind of quarterback. But he gets the job done just as well.

I'm going to miss Glenn, now that he is with Seattle. I feel fortunate that I've had the chance to play with some very good quarterbacks through the years: Boomer, Bubby, Neil, Frank, Glenn, and now Vinny.

They're all super guys. They've all helped me along the way.

I had played against Curtis Martin twice a year for the last three years, so I knew, coming in, what kind of player he was. He's a great running back. He's smart, he's heady, and he's got a great work ethic. Curtis also catches the ball well and runs very good routes for a running back, which adds another dimension to our passing game.

One of his best qualities is that he will do whatever it takes to help his team win. If he's got to block, he's going to block. He always wants to carry the ball—and you've got to like that attitude—but he knows he's got to do whatever the play calls for.

Having a fullback like Keith Byars is also a big help to our running game and the offense in general. Keith can still pack a wallop. He proved that in our win over Carolina when he caught the ball in the flat and he turned upfield. Kevin Greene, the Panthers' veteran linebacker and part-time pro wrestler, was waiting for him at the two-yard line, and Keith just put his head down and mangled him. Kevin ended up leaving the game with a concussion and a big lump on his forehead.

In 1998, Keith and I sat together in all of the team meetings, so we talked all the time. Every day we would each come in with trivia questions or brainteasers. We covered any topic—from "How many keys on a piano?" to "How many teeth in the human mouth?"

A typical brainteaser might be:

A cowboy rides into town on Sunday. He stays three days, and he leaves on Sunday. How is that possible?
Answer: The horse's name is Sunday.

There was one stretch where I would pose the same type of questions to Keith for five days straight, beginning with: "Who holds the record for all-time catches by a running back?" And he'd pretend to struggle with it, saying, "Ooo! That's a tough one."

It was Keith, of course.

Just sitting there doing brainteasers with one of your teammates is part of what camaraderie is all about. So was the little ritual I had going the past three seasons with fellow receiver Alex Van Dyke, who is now with the Pittsburgh Steelers. We would always go out on the field before the rest of the team to throw the ball around together. We'd run some quick routes or we'd have some imaginary plays, using the camera guys as defenders. I'd play quarterback and whisper the call to Alex, maybe send him in motion out of the backfield or whatever. Then I'd throw him the ball and we'd pretend we had just scored the winning touchdown against that day's opponent.

If you feel close enough to someone where he becomes

like a brother to you, when you're on that field, you take offense to anyone hitting him a little too hard or getting in his face. When you love the people you're playing next to, you're going to have a really passionate team and you're going to do well, no matter whom you're playing against.

Bryan Cox is another veteran who has helped build the camaraderie we have on the field and in the locker room.

Some people who only think of him as a troublemaker might find that surprising. And Bryan has caused his share of trouble. He gets fines and brings a lot of controversy to himself because of some of the things he says and some of the confrontations he has had with opposing players, fans, and the NFL.

I didn't know what to expect from having Bryan as a teammate. But when I first saw him on the field for us, I just saw a highly motivated, highly emotional player. And that becomes contagious.

Bryan is still a hell of a linebacker, which I already knew from playing against him when he was with Miami and Chicago. The guy hits as hard as anybody does in the league.

The funniest quote I ever heard about Bryan came from a friend of mine, Jay Mohr, an actor who played the part of rival agent Bob Sugar in the movie *Jerry Maguire*. Jay, who grew up in Verona, New Jersey, is a die-hard Jets fan. We met one night at a Nets' game, and after we signed Bryan, Jay called me from the West Coast and said, "He's not the fastest guy and it may take him a while to get there. But when he gets there, he's angry."

That sums up Bryan to a T. He's not a superfast linebacker like a Hardy Nickerson of Tampa Bay. But when he gets to the ballcarrier, he's definitely bringing it. Hard.

Sometimes Bryan's emotions get the best of him, but that doesn't mean he's a bad person. In fact, I think he's a great guy.

Whenever Bryan sees me, he says, "What's up, little shit?" I'll say something just as insulting back to him, if not more so, and rather than try to kill me, he just laughs.

In practice, if we're running through zones, sometimes he's the first guy covering me. I always just sneak around him, of course, and sometimes I might even give him a quick shot to his side and knock him down. I'll start laughing and he'll get up yelling, "Come here, you little shit!"

It's all in fun and we have a great mutual respect. But I know that one of these days, Bryan's going to get me back.

He just has to catch me first.

Before the 1998 season, Todd Haley, one of our offensive assistant coaches, gave me a highlight tape of the San Francisco 49ers' offense.

He figured that if we were going to put a certain kind of route into our offense, the tape would help show different ways to run it against different kinds of defenses. And who better to learn from than Jerry Rice?

There are a lot of reasons to study Jerry, of course. Number one, because he does things in the worst possible conditions. Because with the obvious attention on him, he's going to get double-teamed most of the time. So if you're ever going to see how to run a route correctly, he's going to show you how to do it. And he's not going to always run the same route. He's going to improvise, too.

There are any number of ways to get to the point where that ball's going to be. It might take fifty different routes—in and out; out and in; come off the line hard; come off the line soft—but he's going to get there.

Then, when you see in a game how a defense is playing you and you remember what worked when you saw Jerry against that same defense, you know that's the way to run it. Don't try to force the issue. If you saw it work for him, it will usually work for you.

Now, obviously, Jerry's the best and there are things he can do—athletically—that other receivers can't. But if you pay close attention to the way he positions himself and controls his body, there are always helpful techniques you can pick up.

I also make a point of looking at tapes of Buffalo's offense, so I can study Andre Reed, another of the great receivers in the game. Because we play the Bills twice a year, there is a pretty hefty tape library from which to choose.

I try to have a comparable style to Andre's, because he seems to have the whole package as far as receivers go. He blocks really well, he runs deep routes well, he runs across the middle, he takes hits. There is really no weakness in his game.

I wouldn't care if I was a twelve-year vet, if I saw a rookie running a route a certain way that I thought could enhance my game, I wouldn't hesitate to try it. You can always learn something from somebody. You can never know too much.

Powerful football ability only takes you so far. The longer

you play and your tendencies become known, the more you need to add different wrinkles to make your ability that much better.

But even if you borrow little things here and there, ultimately every receiver develops his own style. For instance, a lot of times when I'm running a quick out from the slot—which is the pattern I probably run the most—I'm going from the inside out. And as soon as I catch the ball, if I feel the guy covering me is going to run past me, I automatically spin back inside, where I'm pointing straight upfield, whereas most receivers tend to turn the other way. If the defender anticipates that I'm going to turn to the outside, he'll overrun me and I can get a tremendous amount of extra yards.

I've had other players ask, "Why do you do spin inside?" I have no clue. I never think about doing it. I just do it.

And as long as it keeps working, I'm going to continue to do it.

13

It Only Hurts When You Kick It

I think it occurred to me in our first game that 1998 was going to be a breakout season for us.

We opened in San Francisco and the game turned into a toe-to-toe shootout between Glenn Foley and Steve Young. Although we lost, 36–30, in overtime, I think our performance showed what kind of team we were going to have, especially on offense.

Going into the game, no one outside our locker room expected us to have much of a chance to win. It was Jerry Rice's comeback game. It was San Francisco's home opener. We were traveling across the country.

But even with all of that working in the Niners' favor, it took what NFL Films would later describe as the greatest run in league history—Garrison Hearst's amazing ninety-six-yard touchdown carry—to beat us in OT.

I'm not saying any of us had a reason to feel happy after that game: You're never happy after a loss. But I could think of four hundred and fifteen reasons to feel encouraged. That was Foley's total passing yards for the day. I had a hundred and twenty-five and a touchdown on six catches; Keyshawn Johnson had a hundred and twenty-six and two touchdowns on nine catches.

From that first game on, Glenn—and later, Vinny—constantly preached that we had a good enough offense to do something big as a team right away, in 1998, rather than sometime down the road. They did what good quarterbacks are supposed to do—they took control and showed us the way.

The coaches started using the receivers differently than they had the year before. In '97, they wanted to put us in a position where we could do what we did the best. So if you ran certain types of routes better than others, those were the routes they wanted you to run the most. In my case, it was crossing routes, and that meant I was usually in the slot and entering games on third down. I made only one start, which came against Chicago when Jeff Graham was hurt.

But in 1998, we switched it up so that we didn't have the

same tendencies that opponents could key on. Keyshawn ran a lot more crossing routes than he had previously. With Jeff being traded to Philadelphia during the '98 draft, I was back to being a full-time starter and I began going deep a little bit more than I did in my first three seasons. Then you add the great outside speed of Dedric Ward into the mix to back off the defense, and things opened up for all of us.

Dedric can catch the inside routes, too, but until they can cover him on the deep route, we're going to keep throwing it.

Being a backup during those previous two years was tough. You'd go into the season ready to kill for your team. Then, the next thing you know, you're on the sideline for half the game.

It can get kind of demoralizing at times.

Bill had told me, as well as the media, that because I had spent most of the previous two years as a reserve, he was concerned about my ability to thrive in the starting role. That was Bill just trying to push my buttons—trying to challenge me, get a little charge out of me.

I told him that I had played almost every down in my first two years, and I had even returned punts in my second year. It's all a matter of perception. Since Bill came to the Jets, I had been a situational player. But the fact was, I had started my first year and a half and I had never seemed to have any trouble with it. In fact, I felt I had excelled in a worse situation because sometimes I was the only receiver on the field drawing attention from the defense. Now I had Keyshawn and Dedric, as well as Curtis Martin's running and receiving.

As for Parcells, I had come through for him already. He knew, at clutch time, I would come through for him again.

Because of the faith our coaches had in Curtis, who had been a great weapon for them in New England, we entered the season deciding we were going to run the ball more than we had in the past. Even if Curtis didn't happen to produce big yards, as was the case early on, we would still keep running him.

And when you're trying to pound the ball like that, the receivers do more blocking, which is perfectly fine with me. I like to block. I'm not going to say I'm the best blocker in the world, but I'll put every bit as much effort into that as I put into catching the ball. Sometimes I'm at a disadvantage because when I'm in the slot, I'm called upon to block safeties, outside linebackers, and defensive ends. I could be cracking guys who weigh 285 to 300 pounds. I'd like to knock everybody down every chance I get, but when you weigh 185 pounds, that's not always going to be possible.

I remember the time in 1996 when we were playing against Oakland and I hit Jerry Ball, the 350-pound defensive tackle who now plays for Minnesota. The defensive end that I was supposed to block had taken himself out of the play, so I had to hit somebody and I would up colliding with Ball. It was like: *You've got to be kidding me.* I felt like I had just smacked into a concrete building. There are just some guys I'm not ever going to be able to budge, and Ball's one of them. But I'm still going to try to get in their way and aggravate the hell out of them so they can't make the tackle.

Besides, I don't have to exactly win the block; I just have to make sure I don't lose it. When you've got a running back like Curtis, all you have to do is hold up your guy for a second, give Curtis a little hole, and you've done your job.

If we have a running play called in a bump-and-run situation, we're trying to make it look like a pass pattern by coming off fast to just get the defense to back off a little, rather than giving away the fact we're going to run by coming off the line slow and blocking. And if we can sell the opposite of what we're trying to do, great, but still the most important thing is getting the guy you're responsible for out of the play.

When a team is as willing to keep pounding the ball on the ground as we were in '98, it can do wonders for your passing game. At certain points if we were running well, defenses had to bring seven or eight guys in the box to try to stop us.

When that happened, we knew there were some vacant areas to throw the ball, and our quarterbacks usually found them.

After losing to Baltimore in Week Two, we started to hear rumblings from media and fans about us being the "same old Jets." That was what Bill warned us was going to happen after the game, as only he could do, in our solemn dressing room. A lot of things went wrong that day, including a rib injury that Foley suffered in the third quarter.

We needed to do something big in our third game, against Indianapolis. And with Vinny starting at quarterback, we did—with a 44–6 victory. You knew what kind of day it was going to be when, on Vinny's first pass in a Jets' uniform, he threw a screen that Leon Johnson took eighty-two yards for a touchdown, the first of four Vinny would throw that afternoon. Our offense generated five hundred and five yards, including three hundred and two on the ground.

The last time the Jets had that kind of output, I was fifteen.

It would have been nice to celebrate our first win of the season in a big way, but I couldn't. I was too busy wondering whether I would play another game that year.

I thought my season had come to an abrupt end with a freak injury I suffered early in the third quarter. With the game well in hand, we had a second-and-five and I caught a six-yard quick out. Simple play. No big deal.

But as I continued out of bounds after the catch, I got a sudden and horrible surprise when I noticed the guy holding the first-down chain hadn't dropped it. In fact, he started to pull on it and in so doing, he lifted the chain about two feet off the ground. I tried jumping over it, but as I came down, I kind of clipped it and upon landing my left ankle turned in so far that the bone actually hit the ground.

The last time my ankle hurt as much as it did at that moment was when I had broken it during that summer basketball camp when I was in high school. My first thought was, *This season's over for a while.* My second thought was to go after the guy that had lifted the chain, but I was hurting too much to do anything other than hobble over to the wall and hang on until the trainers arrived. (I would later find out that the chain guy was a substitute—the regular had had a death in his family—and he felt so bad afterward, he called the Jets all week to apologize.)

The next thing I knew, I was taking the first cart ride off the field of my NFL career. That was when my parents, my sister, and Amy became very worried. They know, at all costs, I'm walking off after an injury. But no matter how hard I closed my eyes or bit my lip, that wasn't going to happen this time.

As soon as I got inside the locker room, I was given a painkilling shot and an anti-inflammatory pill.

X rays would show that my ankle wasn't broken after all. Dr. James Nicholas, our team physician, would explain that because the tendons had been stretched out so much from previous injuries, there was enough flexibility to keep the bones from snapping. I know I should have been thankful to hear all of that, but my ankle seemed to be telling a far less optimistic story.

An hour later, I was still in agony.

I told Dr. Nicholas that there was no way I was going to miss our next game—against Miami—or any game, for that matter. He just told me to relax. Fortunately, we had a bye coming up, which would give me extra time to heal.

During the fourth quarter, Dad, Mom, Jen, and Amy came down to the entrance of the locker room to check on me. When they saw me hobbling out on crutches, with my ankle packed in ice and wrapped with an Ace bandage, you would have never guessed that only a short distance away our favorite team was putting the finishing touches on a thirty-eight-point victory. They were all upset, but I assured them that everything would be OK. At least that was what I was trying to portray on the outside.

Inside, I didn't have a clue when I would feel better again.

I skipped our usual postgame dinner as a family, stopped by my apartment in Hackensack, and headed straight for Hempstead to begin immediate treatment, just to prevent the swelling from getting out of control. But my ankle had already blown up like a balloon and turned dark purple. Working with our trainer, Dave Price, I stayed there until midnight.

"How bad is it?" I asked Dave.

"Pretty bad."

"How long are we looking at?"

"It all depends on what happens in the first forty-eight hours."

"Look, I've got to play in that Miami game."

Dave didn't really give me an answer. He didn't want to get my hopes up, but he also didn't want to say, "No way."

I was back at eight the next morning and, over the next two weeks, would keep coming back, twice a day, for treatment. I was one of the only players around for most of that first week because just about everyone else left town to take advantage of the few days we were going to have off from practice because of the bye.

It was so ironic, because I'm rarely in the trainer's room, even on a social basis. And every time I'd go in there after my ankle injury, I'd say, "I hate this freakin' place! No offense to you trainers, but I'd rather be anywhere else in the world right now." I had always prided myself on staying out of the trainer's room since the very first time I heard a veteran teammate utter the phrase: "You can't make the club in the tub."

A lot of pain is mental. Up to that point in my NFL career, I had had injuries that caused me to miss a couple of practices, but never a game. Shall we review my football-related medical history? Let's see: Arthroscopic surgery on both shoulders and on one of my knees; multiple concussions, mostly suffered in college; torn rib cartilage; severely sprained collarbone and ankles; hip pointers; all kinds of jammed fingers.

I think I also hold the NFL record for most forearm turf burns. By the end of the season, there is hardly any skin left on either one, only scabs.

I've just always believed that if you don't want to be hurt, you won't be hurt. Unless you've torn a ligament in your knee or have a broken bone or something wrong with your neck, I honestly think that you can ignore pain and keep playing. That doesn't make me special. The majority of guys in the NFL play hurt. It just comes down to a basic question: How much pain can you withstand? I think I have a pretty high threshold, myself, just from the way I handled the many calamities my body has been through since childhood.

But that doesn't set me far apart from a lot of my teammates or anyone else in this game, past or present.

• • •

During our first bye-week practice, I was standing on the sidelines in my sweats, with my ankle in an air cast and hooked to a portable electro-stimulator to help speed the healing process.

All of a sudden, out of nowhere, I felt someone's foot kick the inside of my left ankle from behind. Although it was the outside that I injured, the vibration from the kick had me seeing stars.

I spun around and saw that it was none other than Bill Parcells.

"What's wrong with you?" I asked.

"Did it hurt?"

"No, it felt good. Do it again . . . Yeah, it hurt!"

Then he just walked away.

As I told some reporters afterward, if I could have put pressure on my left foot, I would have used my right foot to kick him right in his ass. And I wasn't kidding.

When my comments were relayed to Bill, he told reporters that if I had kicked him, it would have been the biggest mistake of my life. I don't think he was kidding, either.

I can laugh about it now, but at the time, I was pretty pissed off. Bill said it was his way of testing how close I was to coming back and that it would be more accurate than asking me how I felt because, being the competitor I am, I would probably lie and say I was OK. A week or so earlier, he had sneaked up behind Foley and gave his damaged rib cage a squeeze. When Glenn let out a yelp, that told Bill he still wasn't ready to come back.

I wonder if the American Medical Association is up on these sophisticated methods of diagnosis?

Here I was treating this thing every day, six hours a day, and the last thing I needed was to have my coach, of all people, kick it and possibly set me back a couple of days. Are you kidding me? Fortunately, that wasn't the case.

A lot of the reason for the exchange between Bill and I stems from the fact both of us are from Bergen County. Bergen County natives have the same kind of mind-set. You never let somebody crap on you. It's just the mentality of people there that you stand up to anyone who tries to wrong you in any way.

No, it wasn't all right that he kicked me, even if he was the head coach, so I let him know about it. And his typical, Bergen County-like reaction was: "Go ahead, try to kick me back. It will be the last thing you ever do."

Even though I was still pretty far from full recovery, I got the OK to play against the Dolphins—provided I continued to wear the air cast. We won, 20–9, snapping a four-game losing streak to Miami and a seven-game losing streak to Dan Marino. I made it through the entire game, although my contributions were limited by the fact I could barely move at times.

I hated every second that my ankle was in that air cast. I don't even want to get my ankles taped, let alone have something like that on. For that matter, I don't wear any pads on my arms, my thighs, my knees, or my butt. I have no tape on my fingers or on my wrists. I don't wear a mouthpiece anymore. I wore one in high school and college and I tried to wear one in my rookie year in the NFL, but I just didn't feel comfortable with it.

I don't even wear a cup.

Basically, I don't wear a whole lot else under my uniform besides the NO EXCUSES, JUST RESULTS T-shirt that, for superstitious reasons, I only have on for games. All I wear for protection are my helmet and my shoulder pads.

But I didn't have a choice with the air cast. Dave said if I didn't wear it, I couldn't play. He had me there, because he knew how much it meant for me to keep playing. I take a lot of pride in the fact I've been on the field for every one of the sixty-four regular-season and two playoff games the Jets have played during my NFL career.

Maybe I should have waited out another week with the ankle, but we were playing Miami and it was a big game and you have to make sacrifices. I'm not looking for a pat on the back. But I knew I was getting paid whether I played or not, and I just couldn't handle sitting down, watching my teammates play, if there was even the slightest chance for me to be out there with them.

That's just me. I don't like taking shortcuts.

Our lowest point of the 1998 season was our fourth game, in St. Louis, where we suffered a 30–10 loss to drop our record to 2–3.

Telling you why we lost that day is simple. We turned the ball over five times. Foley was back in the lineup after missing two games, but he was replaced by Vinny with three minutes

left after completing only five passes and throwing three interceptions.

What I still can't explain is why, as an entire team, we
weren't ready to play against the Rams.

Bill couldn't figure it out, either. But he damn sure expected us to show him that we had no intention of taking the
same approach to our next game, at New England, on "Monday Night Football."

Apparently, we didn't do a good enough job with that, either. Because with about an hour left in practice the Friday before the game, Bill—who had been even more surly than usual
as he stomped around Weeb Ewbank Hall all week—just suddenly walked off the field and went inside. His assistants followed him, as did the trainers, leaving fifty-three guys looking
at each other and wondering what the hell was going on.

Being the veteran leader that he is, Pepper Johnson finally
assumed the role of player-coach and ran the rest of the
workout.

Later, Parcells told reporters his walkout wasn't meant to
be a form of motivation. "I was just disgusted. I was sick of
looking at it," he said. "I don't want to waste my time. And
that's what I was doing there. . . . I was just leaving."

But if it really was just a little trick to try to light a fire under our ass, it worked. I have to say, for those final sixty minutes, everyone seemed a lot more focused and attentive to his
assignments.

Considering this was the Jets' first appearance on "Monday Night Football" since 1992, a majority of the guys on our
team—including yours truly—had never played on a Monday

night, so it was intense. We had played some Sunday night games, but this was Monday night. This was prime time. I was excited. It was a big game and my boy, Boomer, was up in the box, no doubt looking to tell the nation all kinds of great things about his buddies in green and white.

I've always loved playing under the lights, going back to Hofstra, where we almost always played on Friday night. It's a great atmosphere. People are all nice and liquored-up and crazy in the stands by kickoff.

Bill might have had just a little extra incentive that night—facing the team he had guided for four seasons and that he departed with a lot of hard feelings on both sides—so we understood how big a win would have been for him. We also knew, going into the season, the Patriots were picked by a lot of so-called experts as the team to beat not only in the AFC East, but in the AFC. They had won four games in a row and we had had a letdown the week before, so we had to come out and save some face.

And we did, beating the Pats, 24–14.

Vinny showed why the starting quarterback job would be his for the rest of the season, throwing for two hundred and ninety-four yards and three touchdowns.

Six days later, Curtis had his fourth straight hundred-yard game and our defense just pummeled forty-four-year-old Steve DeBerg, who became the oldest modern-era NFL starter at any position when he took over for injured quarterback Chris Chandler, in our 28–3 win over Atlanta.

No one would have ever guessed that day that the Falcons would go on to win the NFC championship.

Then we took our 4–3 record into a driving rainstorm in Kansas City and pulled out a 20–17 victory on a thirty-two-yard field goal at the final gun by John Hall, our surfer-dude kicker who came to us from Florida via the University of Wisconsin.

The footing was slippery, but you could handle it if you were smart. In those conditions, you want to make sure you keep a low center of gravity, keep your feet under you, and don't try to cut on a dime. To me, the footing wasn't as tough as seeing the ball, which was obscured by the thick sheet of rain in the lights.

Still, I had a couple of catches in that last drive to help set up the winning field goal. With about a minute left, on third-and-three from the Kansas City thirty-six, I came in motion and ran a quick out for six yards, jumping to grab the ball up by my facemask as cornerback Mark McMillan tried to yank it out. Then, with twenty-five seconds to go, on second-and-eight, I just kind of sat in the zone, Vinny found me, and I turned upfield for a nine-yard gain to the nineteen, giving me my third six-catch game of the season. That brought the clock to sixteen seconds.

After a short run by Curtis and an encroachment penalty on the Chiefs, Hall—who had missed two earlier field goals in the game—banged through the points that gave us our third straight win and improved Vinny's record as a starter to 5–0.

Another Heisman Trophy-winning quarterback who enjoyed a fantastic comeback in '98 was Doug Flutie, who was supposed to be a backup after signing with the Bills from the CFL and then wound up going on a magical run after Rob Johnson suffered a rib injury.

Sound familiar?

But Flutie had his magic carpet pulled out from under him by our defense as we rolled to a 34–12 victory over Buffalo that pushed Vinny's record as a starter to 6–0.

Bill Belichick, our assistant head coach, is brilliant when it comes to putting together a defensive game plan, and he was at his very brightest that day. He just stifled Flutie with a blitzing, 4–4–3 alignment that the Bills hadn't seen before and couldn't figure out. Because of Flutie's great mobility, Belichick had his guys concentrate on keeping him in the pocket while using a "spy," linebacker James Farrior, to follow Doug's every twitch.

It was weird how Belichick put this scheme together, sometimes even having a linebacker at safety. It didn't look very sound, but it was, as Flutie threw for a season-low one hundred and fifty-four yards and no touchdowns. He was intercepted twice, sacked twice, and ran three times for only two yards.

When offensive or defensive players look out of synch, it isn't always because they're not ready to play. Maybe you've practiced against something all week, and all of a sudden you come out and the defense or offense is doing something you've never seen before.

I've got a lot of respect for Belichick. He's a brilliant football mind. He eats, sleeps, and drinks football (although the night before the Buffalo game, Flutie Flakes frosted cereal was being served in the defensive meeting). We get along great, although he does have a little vendetta against me in practice. Whenever I'm out there, Belichick makes it a point to double-team me because he can't take losing, even in practice. Before we run a third-down play, he will actually say to me, "I'm going to double you."

I'll say, "Bill, it's only practice."

"I don't give a shit. I'm not going to watch you make a catch and then have myself get yelled at when we watch the tape for not covering you."

And this is during the offensive period. It's not even the defensive period, when his guys are working on the stuff that they're going to use against the next opponent, yet it still bothers him. He's just a very competitive guy.

After the St. Louis game, the next-most frustrating loss of the regular season was when we had our four-game winning streak ended by the Colts, 24–23, in Indianapolis. I think overconfidence got the best of us as we blew a 23–10 halftime lead and let Peyton Manning, the top overall pick of the '98 draft, beat us with a fourteen-yard touchdown pass to tight end Marcus Pollard with twenty-four seconds left.

Parcells was so mad after that one, he threw a laundry bag across the visitor's locker room in the RCA Dome. I was just thankful he wasn't looking for any ankles to kick.

"This is as disappointed as I've been since I've been here," Bill told reporters. "It damn makes me sick."

It made all of us pretty ill. It was definitely a game we should not have lost, and everyone knew it. But I've been on a 1–15 team, and I know the difference between the kind of club we had then and the kind of club we have now. It wasn't like any of us were saying, "Here we go again."

It was more like: "We're better than this."

And everybody just sort of looked at each other in that locker room with a feeling like: *You're damn right we're better than this. Let's go out and run harder, let's lift harder, let's study our playbook harder. Let's be the team we all knew we could be when the season started.*

As far as I was concerned, the moment we walked off the field after the Colts' game was the moment our team launched itself on our championship-style finish, winning the final six games of the season and capturing the AFC East title.

Now I know there are those who believe we actually went 5–1 because they count our 32–31 victory over Seattle as a loss that bad officiating turned into a win. But let me give you my perspective on that game. Keep in mind, it is a Jets' perspective, but then what else were you expecting from a book with a guy in a Jets' uniform on the cover? A Seahawks' slant?

Get real.

Let's set the stage. We had a fourth-and-goal from the Seattle five, the Seahawks were clinging to a 31–26 lead, and we called our third and last timeout with twenty-seven seconds left.

Gathered with the offense on the sidelines, I couldn't believe my ears when I heard Vinny tell Parcells that he wanted to run a quarterback sneak. Parcells couldn't believe it, either.

"I'm telling you," Vinny said, "I can make it."

I said to myself, *You've got to be kidding me. Talk about your ballsy calls!* Now Vinny's a big strong guy, but what he was proposing to do was the kind of thing you probably wouldn't ask Jerome Bettis or even Earl Campbell to do. Because he would be going right through the line. He wasn't going to try to run around it. He was going to take it right up the gut, right into the teeth of a pretty good Seattle defense, five long yards to the end zone.

But at that point of the game, even Bill had to conclude that it was as good an option as any. So after going back and forth on the headsets with the other coaches, he finally said to Vinny, "If you think you can do it, do it."

It was crazy and brilliant at the same time. Crazy because even a supermobile quarterback is going to have a hell of a time trying to reach the end zone under those circumstances, let alone Vinny, who is not exactly Flutie-like as a scrambler. Brilliant because who in their right mind would ever expect a call like that? I'm sure it wasn't high on the Seahawks' list of our offensive tendencies in that situation.

When he stepped up to the line, Vinny actually had two plays to choose from, and he had the option of calling either one, using their respective numbers in our audible system. One number was for the sneak, which was the play he intended to call, and the other was for a pass, which he could switch to in case he didn't like something he saw in the defense or just had a change of heart at the last second.

We were spread out in five wides, with no one in the

backfield. I was in the slot to Vinny's right. And sure enough, he called the number for the sneak.

The excitement was building inside of me. I mean, I was just bursting because I knew he was going to run it himself. And it seemed like we were up there for ten minutes, waiting for the snap. As usual, Vinny looked left and right before he took the ball. When he looked to his right, I caught his eye with an expression that said: *Good luck, pal! Because there's nothing I'm going to be able to do for you on this one.*

And there wasn't. Being in the slot, I was too far away to block anyone that had a shot at being in on the tackle of a play like that. All Vinny was going to do was take the snap and take off behind our center, Kevin Mawae, who had been a Seahawk in the previous four seasons.

So after the snap, I kind of took a few steps forward across the goal line and just kept looking to my left to watch this thing unfold. I remember seeing someone grab Vinny's left leg from behind as he made his dive toward the end zone. I could see that part of his body was over the goal line, but I honestly didn't know whether he was in or not because when he hit the ground, his back was to me and the ball was hidden.

I did see the official on my side, head linesman Ernie Frantz, briefly lift his arms to signal a touchdown, although I'm not sure how he came to that conclusion because he had the same view as I did. So I immediately ran up to him and yelled, "You saw it! You called it! Call it again! Put your hands up!"

Then everyone on our team started screaming and yelling, "Make the call! Make the call! You saw it! He's in! Touch-down! Touchdown!"

We were lobbying so hard, you'd have thought we were in Washington, D.C. I knew the guy thought he saw something to our benefit, so I was just doing whatever I could to make sure he stuck with that. This was an important game; we needed to win it. And now, whether we won or lost, was completely out of our hands.

It was all up to the officials.

Finally Frantz reaffirmed his touchdown call. Jets win! (I have to remember to send him a Christmas card this year.)

I know there are a lot of people who say Vinny was down a good foot before the goal line. I know the Seahawk players and coaches were going nuts—and probably still are—claiming they had been the victims of one of the all-time great robberies in NFL history. I know that the controversy surrounding that play, along with several other controversial calls during the '98 season, had a lot to do with the return of instant replay for 1999.

But as far as I'm concerned, looking at it from a Jet perspective, it was a great call. And I've made a point of not watching any of the zillion replays of it on television, just so I won't prejudice my view.

I don't feel bad or the least bit guilty. It was a win—a big win, a huge win. When you look at the list of games we played in '98, there's a W next to the Seattle game. It doesn't say anything about us not deserving it because of a bad call. It just says W, and that's all that matters.

And you know what? Through the years, enough bad calls have gone against us that we finally deserved to get one in our favor. We went through a similar situation in 1997 in Miami when an official said my six-yard catch on fourth-and-five from the Dolphins' thirty wasn't a catch late in the game. I caught the ball from Foley, I went down, and as I was lying there, a Miami defender bopped it away. The officials ruled it was no catch, even though I had taken three or four steps with the ball. We lost the game, 24–17.

There was nothing we could do about it—then or now—just as there is nothing the Seahawks could do.

Our only focus after the Seattle game was winning the AFC East. With a 9–4 record, we were two W's away.

We got the first one when we beat the Dolphins, 21–16, and clinched our first playoff berth since 1991 under the Sunday night lights and some pretty hostile conditions in Pro Player Stadium. As I was catching five passes for a hundred and five yards and a touchdown, my family was catching grief up in the stands from some frustrated Dolphin fans. Jen got hit in the face with a football and she and my parents had some peanuts whipped at them the whole night.

I went into that game feeling very loose and upbeat. I had gotten myself psyched by going to a movie that afternoon with my father. We saw *The Water Boy*, which thoroughly cracked me up because I'm a big fan of Adam Sandler. Another thing that I'm sure helped me that night was taking a swig of some of that "high-quality H_2O" we had on our sidelines. I'm sure Adam's character would have been pleased.

The next stop was Buffalo, where a win over the Bills would give us an 11–4 record and the division crown.

Talk about your weird circumstances. While President Clinton was in the midst of being impeached, we were in the middle of losing every statistical battle we could to the Bills. They generated three hundred and sixty-six yards to our two hundred and sixty-nine. They produced twenty-one first downs to our fourteen. They converted 47 percent of their third downs to our 20 percent. They had seventy-four offensive plays to our fifty-one. They held the ball 32:47 to our 27:13.

Of course, the only numbers that mattered were the final ones on the scoreboard in Ralph Wilson Stadium: Jets 17, Bills 10.

After Bobby Hamilton and I gave Parcells the first Gatorade shower that I believe any coach in Jets' history had ever had, Bill still had some moisture in his eyes when he got to the locker room. It wasn't from the Gatorade. He was truly emotional about that win and made a point of letting everyone know how much we deserved it, considering the fact that we had just beaten two tough division opponents on the road within a span of six days. Counting New England, we had beaten three AFC East teams in their parks and had won five crucial AFC road games, including trips to Kansas City and Tennessee.

Still, winning the division and clinching the number-two seed in the playoffs behind Denver were only a first step. We knew it wasn't our ultimate goal, which was to make the Super Bowl and win the Super Bowl. But as I've said, I live for the moment. And the moment that clock ticked down and we knew we had captured the AFC East—becoming the last team from the 1970 NFL–AFL merger to win a division title—was very satisfying.

So was closing our regular season at home with a 31–10 win over the Patriots in a game that wasn't supposed to mean anything to us. Except it did mean a lot. The 12–4 record gave us the winningest season in Jets' history. And we had a great running start into the postseason.

We game-planned and practiced for the Patriots just like it was a regular game, as if we needed it to make the playoffs. Winning's contagious and so is losing.

You never want to practice bad habits out there.

A few days after our second win over Miami, the Pro Bowl teams were announced. I'm proud of the fact that four of our guys made it: Vinny, Keyshawn, Aaron Glenn, and Mo Lewis, one of our outstanding linebackers. I congratulate them all.

I'd be lying if I said it didn't hurt a little not to be chosen along with them, but when two guys on the same team, playing the same position, have strong seasons, it almost splits the vote.

But I have absolutely nothing to feel bad about. It was a hell of a year for me. I had almost eleven hundred yards in receptions and eight touchdowns, which were both career highs. I had a good yards-per-catch average at 14.4, and I shared with Keyshawn the league lead in first-down catches with sixty. Plus, I was on a winning team.

Although I already felt a sense of respect from my peers in the league, maybe 1998 was my breakout year where I have got complete respect now.

A lot of people came up to me after the results of the voting by players, coaches, and fans came out and said, "You should have made it." Players and coaches from other teams, guys I really respect in this league, told me that they had voted for me. I appreciated hearing that.

But there are a lot of guys in the league that should have made it. Why focus on the fact that I didn't? Who's to say that I'm more deserving than anybody else is? You could say, yeah, my numbers are better than some of the guys that made it, but I'll be the first one to tell you that numbers don't tell the whole story. Whether you have eleven hundred yards in receptions or you're five-foot-ten, neither one means a thing.

All that matters is what you mean to your team.

Vinny showed the tremendous class he has when he gave Amy and me an all-expenses-paid trip to Hawaii so that we could be with him and his wife, Mitzi, at the Pro Bowl.

Actually, he was staying true to a promise, although I'd have understood if he hadn't in this case. Vinny and I play cards all the time on the plane to road games and in our spare time during the week between games. We play gin all the time and have a set poker game with Foley and Aaron Glenn. And at one point in the season, Vinny said to me, "When you go to the Pro Bowl, you're taking me with you, right?"

I said, "Are you kidding me? You're the one going to the Pro Bowl. You take me."

"All right. If either one of us makes it, we'll take the other one. OK?"

"Sure."

Vinny had already promised Foley he would take him, too. And Keyshawn made the same promise to Foley. And I made the same promise to Foley. So Glenn was getting a free ride to Honolulu somehow.

Amy and I had a great time out there with Vinny and his family. He put us up at the superposh hotel where all of the Pro Bowl players stayed. He shared his time with us. The guy wouldn't even let me pick up a dinner tab.

Of course, it's just a continuation of the tremendous treatment I received from both quarterbacks and their families. The times that I didn't commute to New Jersey during the season, I lived with Glenn and his wife, Jen, who cooked for me all the time. Because so many of the players are married and have children, they take pity on a young bachelor like me who doesn't have a wife and kids of his own to go home to.

Between Jen Foley, Mitzi Testaverde, and Renee Van Dyke, I was very well fed.

As for the Pro Bowl, I think it will come for me in due time. If I really was a good enough player to get there in '98, I'll have the same kind of year in 1999, maybe better.

Besides, I'd much rather make the Super Bowl than the Pro Bowl.

14

"J-E-T-S!"

etting ready for the first playoff game of my NFL career was one of the most incredible experiences of my life.

You could just feel the electricity all around you. And the closer we got to January 10, 1999, for our divisional-round showdown versus Jacksonville in Giants Stadium, the more everyone in the tri-state area was plugged into it.

I would drive into work in the morning, turn on the radio, and there would be Ed Anzalone, the New York fireman who does the "J-E-T-S! Jets! Jets! Jets!" chants at all our home games, on Z-100. Then the next day I would hear him on another station . . . and another. The guy was all over the dial. And he would get himself, the DJs, and the listeners—including the one zipping over to Hempstead from New Jersey with a well-worn Yankees hat on—fired up by doing his chant.

How would you like to wake up to that on your clock radio at the crack of dawn?

All I could think while driving along was: *This is great.* I remembered how much excitement there was all over the place when the Giants would be getting ready for their playoff games. I always wanted to be a part of something like that as a player.

Because it wasn't just about the Jets preparing for a game against an opponent anymore. It was about pride. It was about the whole tri-state area uniting to get behind us, ready to take on all comers. It was bigger than just the team and the players and coaches involved. And it was a super feeling—a feeling that I couldn't ever remember being associated with the Jets in my lifetime.

During our first-round bye, I had been just like any other fan, watching the wild-card games on television. Of course, I had reason to pay closer attention than I had at that point after any of my three previous seasons. Naturally, you do a little sizing up of the possible opponents you're going to meet the following week, but you really save that for the game films. The main thing I found myself looking at was how these teams, especially the ones with postseason experience, handled themselves.

At our next team meeting, Bill Parcells started mentioning some of the specific plays that had hurt the losing teams, and I knew exactly what he was talking about. He told us that at this time of year, the things that send you home right away are turnovers, penalties, and personal fouls—the big things and the little things—and he wanted us thinking about that as we prepared to face the Jaguars. Andre Reed's personal foul and ejection for bumping an official after it was ruled he didn't reach the end zone late in Buffalo's loss to Miami was a classic example of what Bill was talking about. Not having one of the greatest receivers in the game at that point was devastating to the Bills.

The mental part of the game is huge during the season, but it's even larger in the playoffs. Bill kept stressing that he wanted us to be a smart team, reminding us that anything we did—whether it was in the first quarter or the final minutes—could determine the outcome.

I'm not going to lie. When our game started against the Jaguars, it was probably one of the only times in my life that I was on a football field feeling overexcited—to the point where I was almost jittery.

The "J-E-T-S! Jets! Jets! Jets!" chant was ten times louder than it had ever been. There wasn't an empty seat in the house. It was both tremendous and a little overwhelming at the same time.

When you're in the stands, screaming your lungs out with Fireman Ed, that's fine. But feeling that way as a player can be a problem, because you're not focused. Instead of thinking about the game plan and all of the plays and all of your assignments, you just want to go out there and rip somebody's head off.

When you really know there is no tomorrow, the game moves a whole lot faster and the hits are a whole lot harder. At the same time, you keep reminding yourself that there is so much less room for error and that, while the intensity is much greater than usual, you can't allow it to take away from your concentration.

After a couple of plays, I finally calmed down.

Much to my surprise, we made it look pretty easy at the start, taking a 17–0 lead with thirty-three seconds left in the first half after Keyshawn ran a reverse ten yards for a touchdown. But then the Jaguars reminded us why they, too, were a playoff team. Mark Brunell, their dangerous quarterback, threw a bomb that Jimmy Smith caught for a fifty-two-yard touchdown as the half expired.

As easy as it was for us to get going on the Jaguars, it was just as easy for them to turn the game right around on us and suddenly get some momentum. They had the experience when it came to the postseason; a lot of us were fairly new to a game like that. They had been in the playoffs the previous couple of seasons and still had guys on that team who upset Denver on the way to the 1996 AFC Championship Game.

Still, it looked like we were going to cruise to victory when we opened a 31–14 lead in the third quarter.

Sure enough, though, early in the fourth quarter, Brunell

found Smith for a nineteen-yard score. And after linebacker Kevin Hardy's helmet caused me to fumble following an eight-yard catch, Mike Hollis kicked a thirty-seven-yard field goal to pull Jacksonville within 31–24 with about six minutes left.

The fumble had nothing to do with jitters. I was long past the anxiety I had felt at the start of the game. I was just trying to make something extra happen, as I've done my whole career, trying to turn that eight-yard gain into a ten- or fifteen-yarder. Then someone I didn't account for came in and put his helmet on the ball. Stuff like that is going to happen. I just wished it hadn't happened to me at a time like that.

Things got a little more tense for us on the next drive when Donovin Darius picked off Vinny in the end zone. But right after making a big-time play, Donovin made a big-time rookie mistake—he tried to come out of the end zone and was tackled at the one. The Jaguars only got as far as the eight, setting up John Hall's second field goal of the day and sealing our 34–24 victory.

For the first time since 1983, the Jets were in the AFC Championship Game.

Afterward, we were happy in the locker room, but not overjoyed. We just started thinking about Denver, which would be our opponent in seven days in Mile High Stadium. We were excited that we beat the Jaguars, but we still had two more steps before we accomplished our goal.

In fact, after I got back to my apartment in Hackensack—where I lived during the '97 and '98 seasons—that night, I went outside and played basketball with my buddy from college, Brian Clark, who was visiting. It was really cold out, with the temperature in the mid-twenties, so we each put on about five sweatshirts, then went down the street to an outdoor court with lights and shot around for about an hour.

I didn't want to go out and celebrate, because what was there to celebrate? Shooting baskets just seemed a lot more enjoyable to me than anything else I could have been doing.

Traveling to Denver for the AFC Championship Game was an entirely different feeling than facing Jacksonville the previous week. We knew the stakes were higher because we were one step closer. It felt more like a chess match than a football game.

All of us went out there thinking, *No mistakes . . . We have to have pinpoint accuracy . . . We have to do everything to a T.*

We respected the hell out of the Broncos. They were the defending champs. They had the Hall of Fame players. But on January 17, 1999, they were just like us—a team trying to get to the Super Bowl.

Playing at Mile High Stadium—where they were on an eighteen-game winning streak since their playoff loss to Jacksonville two years earlier—was a big advantage for the Broncos. But they deserved it. It was their reward for having the best record in the AFC.

Not only was the crowd revved up to playoff level, as ours had been the week before, but the conditions were something I had never seen before. I'm not talking about the altitude, which bothers a lot of players and teams but wasn't much of an issue that day. I'm talking about a steady twenty-five-to-thirty-mile-an-hour wind that did crazy things to the ball when it was thrown or kicked. You'd try to make a catch over your head and the next thing you'd know, the ball would be between your legs. The wind was all over the place; I couldn't figure it out.

Even Denver's receivers were having problems.

But the day seemed to start off so well. On the opening play of the game, the Broncos were in zone coverage and, after going in motion, I wound up in a familiar place, just sitting in that hole between the corner and the linebacker. Vinny hit me and I turned it up the field for eleven yards. Same thing on the second play, and I picked up fourteen yards.

Then on third-and-six, I ran a seam route. I took the middle of the field because I saw the safeties split wide. All I had to do was get by the underneath guy and I was open. Vinny hit me right in stride for a twenty-eight-yard gain to the Denver twenty-eight. We drove sixty-two yards and it looked like we were on a nonstop flight to the end zone, but then we sputtered. John Hall came out to try a forty-yard field goal, and that crazy wind made us its first victim of the day, causing John's kick to take a right turn away from the uprights like you wouldn't believe.

I mean, it was like a boomerang.

I think that hurt us a lot. Anytime you go down the field like that right off the bat and you've got a defense on its heels, you need to put some points on the board. When you don't, their defense gets an automatic confidence boost, thinking, *All right, we bent, but we didn't break.*

Thanks to a goal-line stand by our defense, we were able to shut out the Broncos in the first half, which was something I'm sure not many people expected. And on the final play of the half, Hall managed to beat the wind with a thirty-two-yard field goal. A 3–0 halftime lead certainly isn't something to brag about, but in the AFC title game, it's huge.

Three minutes into the third quarter, we quieted that roaring crowd even more when Blake Spence, a rookie tight end who hadn't been active for a game since October, blocked Tom Rouen's punt. Fred Baxter recovered at the Denver one and one play later, Curtis was in the end zone to give us a 10–0 lead.

I thought, right there, we could have really put some pressure on them by turning a ten-point lead into a seventeen-point lead and make them start scrambling to get back into the game. When that happens, the opponent starts pressing and making mistakes.

Unfortunately, the mistake-prone team on the field that day was wearing green and white. We lost four fumbles and they were by people, like Keith Byars, whom I had never really seen fumble before. I don't think I even remember seeing Keith fumble all the way back to when he played for Philadelphia.

But I had fumbled a week earlier, under equally critical circumstances, so I don't blame those guys for anything.

Counting a couple of interceptions by Vinny, we wound

up with six turnovers. That just wasn't the type of thing we had been doing for most of the season. And when it happens in the playoffs, the exit door is wide open waiting for you to go home.

We did, after a 23–10 loss.

The Broncos have a great team, but I think on that day it was more a case of us losing than of Denver winning. We had no one else to blame but ourselves. Some days you can play your absolute best and lose. On that day we knew we didn't play our best, myself included.

I finished with eight catches for a hundred and twenty-one yards, my biggest output of the season. But you can always do more, especially on a day when the offense gets into scoring range six times and you only have a touchdown and a field goal to show for it.

I hate talking about this game. I hate to even think about it. I hate talking or thinking about any game we ever lost.

I know a lot of people consider it a great accomplishment to come within a game of the Super Bowl. For me, it wasn't good enough. It'll never be good enough.

I don't play to just come up short.

All of us pretty much did our own thing on that long and mostly quiet flight home from Denver. Some guys watched the movie, while others—including yours truly—played cards.

Just anything you could do to take your mind off of that painful defeat.

We landed at LaGuardia Airport at about two in the morning. And when we got off the plane, I don't think anybody could believe who was on hand to greet us. There, standing at the end of the jetway, was none other than Mr. Leon Hess, shaking hands with every player, coach, and staff member.

Mr. Hess had become too weary to travel to our road games, but even at that late hour, he managed to make it out to the airport to do something that would mean so much to every one of us—something I know I will never forget.

"Thank you for a great season," Mr. Hess said as he grabbed my hand. "We'll get 'em next year."

It was just the kind of thing you wanted—and needed—to hear at that point. I only wish there would be a "next year" for Mr. Hess. But even though we weren't able to get him that second Super Bowl trophy while he was around to enjoy it with us, his being there that night just showed you the kind of character he had.

I'm just thankful that I had the opportunity to play for such a great owner.

Watching the Broncos play in Super Bowl XXXIII was painful. I congratulate them for beating Atlanta and winning back-to-back Lombardi trophies. I congratulate John Elway on a great career that is now all packed up and ready to be shipped to Canton, Ohio. It will be nice to tell my grandchildren someday that I was on the same field with him for his final game in Mile High Stadium.

But our loss is lodged too deep in my throat for me to say much more than that.

Besides, my thoughts are focused on the '99 season, on taking care of unfinished business. That definitely was Parcells's focus in signing free agents such as tight end Eric Green, free safety Steve Atwater, linebacker Roman Phifer, and punter Tom Tupa.

If someone were to come up to me before the '99 season and say, "You guys are going to be good; I'll bet you finish at least 12–4 again," I wouldn't be flattered.

A 12–4 record is good. A 15–1 record is even better. But why would I want to say, right now, that sometime during the course of the season we're going to lose four games or even one game?

I refuse to think that way.

I've never blamed anyone for the road I had to travel to get where I am. Nor will I ever. What am I going to do, hold a grudge against my father because I'm five-foot-ten? That's ridiculous.

How can I complain about anything? I'm healthy and I'm living a dream.

Anytime you think you've got problems, go visit a children's hospital.

I've seen kids who are terminally ill, who are old enough to realize that they're going to die soon, with the biggest and brightest smiles you've ever seen in your life.

You walk out of there with a whole different perspective on what you might ever consider a hardship.

We take for granted that we can walk. We have remote

controls because we don't want to get off the couch to change the channel on the TV set. There are people who would kill to be able to get out of a wheelchair and do that.

Take a stroll around New York sometime. Check out the people who call a cardboard box home, then tell me you've got a problem with where you're living.

You have to step out of yourself every now and then and see what your life looks like through the eyes of someone else. It's all about stopping to smell the roses and being appreciative of what you have and what you've done, rather than worrying about what you don't have and what you haven't done.

I found myself doing that not long after I returned from the Pro Bowl and learned that Vinny's father, Big Al Testaverde, had died of a heart attack. When Vinny's wife called to give me the news, I was in shock. I couldn't believe it. I knew that he had heart problems, but from what I understood, the guy was as strong as an ox. I had also just spent eight days in Hawaii with Vinny and his wife and kids, so we were closer than ever at that point.

I knew how close Vinny was to his father. He had the same relationship with his father that I have with mine. And Al's death made me step back a second and look at my life and see what a great family I have. As often as we're together, I thought about all of the times I could have visited my parents and didn't for one reason or another.

And one of the first times we got together after that, I went out and bought my father a little present. OK, it was a big present: a 1998 candy-apple red Corvette.

It was always something I wanted to do. My father has loved Corvettes his whole life, but he had sold the last one he had. I knew he loved the one I was driving, and now that I was in a position to afford it, I wanted to get him one, too. I wanted to give him something that would make him feel good and also watch him enjoy it.

It wasn't about buying Dad something. It was about showing him just how much I appreciated everything he had ever done for me.

Life is too short. Football careers are even shorter. I think the average playing career in the NFL is three-point-something years. The way I look at it, I've been on borrowed time since my point-one year that wasn't even supposed to happen.

Although 1998 was the best of my first four NFL seasons, I know I can play better. I know I can be a better player tomorrow than I am today.

People say my hands might be up there with those of the best receivers in the league. But I'm still going to go out in practice and try to catch more balls than anybody because I don't want to drop a single one.

Look at Jerry Rice. If anybody's ever going to try to follow in somebody's footsteps, those aren't bad ones to start with. You're looking at the best in the world at what he does, yet this man works harder than anybody in the world at what he does.

And I say that as someone who works pretty damn hard himself.

That sort of work ethic is a reminder that you shouldn't be satisfied with just getting an opportunity to do something with the talent you have. If you're given the opportunity, you might as well take advantage of it.

I'm living proof of what can happen when you do.

Wayne Chrebet's Career Statistics

Wayne Chrebet's Professional
Receiving Statistics

Year	Team	G/S	No.	Yds.	Avg.	LG	TD
1995	N.Y. Jets	16/16	66	726	11.0	32	4
1996	N.Y. Jets	16/9	84	909	10.8	44	3
1997	N.Y. Jets	16/1	58	799	13.8	70	3
1998	N.Y. Jets	16/16	75	1,083	14.4	63t	8
Totals		64/42	283	3,517	12.4	70	18
Playoffs		2/2	12	166	13.8	28	0

Wayne Chrebet's Year-by-Year,
Game-by-Game Statistics

1995 Game-by-Game Receiving

Date	Opponent	No.	Yds.	Avg.	LG	TD
Sept. 3	at Miami	3	43	14.3	27	0
Sept. 10	Indianapolis	2	14	7.0	9	1
Sept. 17	Jacksonville	7	58	8.3	13	1
Sept. 24	at Atlanta	4	56	11.5	32	0
Oct. 1	Oakland	4	46	11.5	18	0

Oct. 8	at Buffalo	7	74	10.6	17	1
Oct. 15	at Carolina	4	56	14.0	13	0
Oct. 22	Miami	3	41	13.7	16	1
Oct. 29	at Indianapolis	3	17	5.7	6	0
Nov. 5	New England	4	66	16.5	32	0
Nov. 19	Buffalo	3	42	14.0	22	0
Nov. 26	at Seattle	1	6	6.0	6	0
Dec. 3	St. Louis	8	98	12.3	26	0
Dec. 10	at New England	4	45	11.3	21	0
Dec. 17	at Houston	3	24	8.0	12	0
Dec. 24	New Orleans	6	40	6.7	9	0

1996 Game-by-Game Receiving

Date	Opponent	No.	Yds.	Avg.	LG	TD
Sept. 1	at Denver	4	20	5.0	7	0
Sept. 8	Indianapolis	7	93	13.3	44	0
Sept. 15	at Miami	6	60	10.0	19	0
Sept. 22	N.Y. Giants	4	31	7.8	14	0
Sept. 29	at Washington	4	63	15.8	25	0
Oct. 6	Oakland	3	28	9.3	17	0
Oct. 13	at Jacksonville	12	162	13.5	32	1
Oct. 20	Buffalo	6	73	12.2	21	1
Oct. 27	Arizona	5	46	9.2	18	0
Nov. 10	New England	3	33	11.0	20	0
Nov. 17	at Indianapolis	3	32	10.7	13	0
Nov. 24	at Buffalo	10	75	7.5	14	0
Dec. 1	Houston	5	41	8.2	14	0
Dec. 8	at New England	4	52	13.0	15	0

| Dec. 14 | Philadelphia | 4 | 59 | 14.8 | 28 | 0 |
| Dec. 22 | Miami | 4 | 41 | 10.3 | 14 | 1 |

1997 Game-by-Game Receiving

Date	Opponent	No.	Yds.	Avg.	LG	TD
Aug. 31	at Seattle	3	73	24.3	35t	2
Sept. 7	Buffalo	3	39	13.0	21	0
Sept. 14	at New England	6	82	13.6	39	0
Sept. 21	Oakland	4	48	12.0	19	0
Sept. 28	at Cincinnati	6	68	11.3	22	0
Oct. 5	at Indianapolis	4	39	9.8	18	0
Oct. 12	Miami	5	104	20.8	70	1
Oct. 19	New England	2	39	19.5	20	0
Nov. 2	Baltimore	5	46	9.2	11	0
Nov. 9	at Miami	4	30	7.5	12	0
Nov. 16	at Chicago	2	12	6.0	8	0
Nov. 23	Minnesota	4	66	16.5	25	0
Nov. 30	at Buffalo	6	86	14.3	30	0
Dec. 7	Indianapolis	0	0	0.0	0	0
Dec. 14	Tampa Bay	0	0	0.0	0	0
Dec. 21	at Detroit	4	67	16.8	33	0

1998 Game-by-Game Receiving

Date	Opponent	No.	Yds.	Avg.	LG	TD
Sept. 6	at San Francisco	6	125	20.8	48	1
Sept. 13	Baltimore	6	91	15.2	24	0
Sept. 20	Indianapolis	3	25	8.3	11	1

Oct. 4	Miami	2	18	9.0	12	0
Oct. 11	at St. Louis	5	42	8.4	13	0
Oct. 19	at New England	5	59	11.8	22	0
Oct. 25	Atlanta	4	54	13.5	17	0
Nov. 1	at Kansas City	6	101	16.8	56	0
Nov. 8	Buffalo	4	58	14.5	22	1
Nov. 15	at Indianapolis	4	112	28.0	63t	1
Nov. 22	at Tennessee	4	38	9.5	15	0
Nov. 29	Carolina	7	107	15.3	36	2
Dec. 6	Seattle	7	74	10.6	23	0
Dec. 13	at Miami	5	105	21.0	52	1
Dec. 19	at Buffalo	3	30	10.0	12	1
Dec. 27	New England	4	44	11.0	16	0

1998–99 Playoffs Receiving

Date	Opponent	No.	Yds.	Avg.	LG	TD
Jan. 10	Jacksonville	4	45	11.2	16	0
Jan. 17	at Denver	8	121	15.1	28	0

Class of '95

Through the 1998 season, Wayne Chrebet ranked second in receptions among all of the wide receivers who entered the NFL in 1995, including thirty-one who were drafted:

Name	Team	Draft Rd.	Rec.	Yds.	Avg.	TD
F. Sanders	Arizona	2	285	3,928	13.8	12
Chrebet	**N.Y. Jets**	**FA**	**283**	**3,517**	**12.4**	**18**
Galloway	Seattle	1	261	4,068	15.6	36
Freeman	Green Bay	3	223	3,623	16.2	36
Stokes	San Francisco	1	174	2,225	12.8	15
Westbrook	Washington	1	146	2,322	15.9	11
C. Sanders	Tennessee	3	119	2,339	19.7	16
Dunn	Pittsburgh	5	83	1,185	14.3	4